DDC

Internet in an Hour: Business Communication and E-Mail

Joy Van Skiver
Kathy Berkemeyer
Don Mayo

Acknowledgements

To my favorite dining partner, Burt.
Joy Van Skiver

Dedicated to the memory of my parents, John and Gert Madden.
Kathy Berkemeyer

Thanks to Jen, Midori, and Monique: We did it!
Don Mayo

Managing Editor	Project Manager	Technical Editors	English Editor	Design and Layout
Jennifer Frew	Scott Isebrand	Jennifer Frew Cathy Vesecky	Monique Peterson	Shawn Morningstar Shu Chen Elviro Padro Paul Wray

Copyright© 1999 by DDC Publishing, Inc.
Published by DDC Publishing, Inc.
The information contained herein is copyrighted by DDC Publishing, Inc.
All right reserved, including the right to reproduce this book or portions thereof in any form whatsoever. For information, address DDC Publishing, Inc., 275 Madison Avenue, 12th Floor, New York, New York 10016
Internet address: *http://www.ddcpub.com*

ISBN: 1-56243-676-7
Cat. No. HR6
10 9 8 7 6 5 4 3 2 1
Printed in the United States of America.

Netscape™, Netscape™ Communications logo, Netscape™ Communications Corporation, Netscape™ Communications, Netscape Mail™, and Netscape™ Navigator are all trademarks of Netscape™ Communications Corporation.
Microsoft® and Windows® are registered trademarks of the Microsoft Corporation.
Yahoo!™ and Yahoo™ logo are trademarks of Yahoo!™
LYCOS™, LYCOS™ logo are trademarks of LYCOS™.
AltaVista™ and the AltaVista™ logo are trademarks of AltaVista Technology, Inc.
Digital™ and the Digital™ logo are trademarks of Digital Equipment Corporation.
Excite is a service mark of Excite Inc
Bigfoot and Bigfoot footprint are service marks of Bigfoot Partners L.P.
Four11 is the property of Four11 Corporation.
Internet Address Finder is the property of DoubleClick Inc.
Switchboard™ is a trademark of Banyan Systems Inc.
WhoWhere?™ and the WhoWhere?™ logo are trademarks of WhoWhere? Inc.
Some illustrations in this book and on the DDC Web site have been acquired from Web sites and are used for demonstration and educational purposes only. Online availability of text and images does not imply that they may be reused without the permission of the copyright holder, although the Copyright Act does permit certain unauthorized reuse as fair use under 17 U.S.C. Section 107

All registered trademarks, trademarks, and service marks are the property of their respective companies.

Preface

- If you're like most of the people I meet at our business writing seminars, you have a few questions about grammar, punctuation and style. Unless there's a writing expert in your office, you probably don't have a good source for answers to those questions.

- Most style guides have an academic or journalistic slant. This book concentrates instead on the kind of writing business professionals do every day. Since I have included only the subjects you need for business, you won't find rules for writing a bibliography, and there aren't any references to poetry or essays.

- I have based The Writing Exchange Business Style Guide on the thousands of questions my staff and I have answered in the last 17 years. Our experience has shown that business professionals are eager to know what's right; they don't want to guess. Because we give explanations in plain English and use business examples, people quickly understand what they never understood in school. Usually, the response we hear is, "Oh, that's why!"

- I'll never forget the person who said, "Joy, the rules are so easy when you're here to explain them. I wish I could carry you around in my pocket so I'll always have the right answer."

- May this "pocket" version of a business writing expert give you all the answers you need.

Thank You

- Any project that requires as much attention to detail as a style guide needs more than one person to keep it on track. I was fortunate to have lots of help.
- Susanne Bassmann was my right hand, and Burt Spielman was my left.
- Susanne worked closely with me on every aspect of this book from my first draft to the final copy. She was a careful editor who offered improvements without destroying my ideas. Her sensitivity to the reader's understanding was extremely valuable as she checked and double-checked and triple-checked every explanation. When tensions were running high, she was also our Manager of Humor and Comic Relief.
- Burt's expertise in desktop publishing made this project feasible. His engineering background was also an asset when we examined grammatical terms. He occasionally reminded me that my readers are not interested in subordinate conjunctions and noun clauses functioning as objects of prepositions. Burt's commitment to work with me on weekends and evenings went beyond the dedication of a staff member; only a loving husband could give so much time and effort to "my" book.
- Phyllis Dresher's reputation for simplifying grammar served us well as she reviewed several early drafts. She identified sections that might have confused our readers and suggested logical ways to break up complex material.
- Although Karin Hayes Callahan joined us late in the project, she quickly became a vital team member as we reviewed and polished the final product. Having a fresh pair of eyes in the last four months was just what we needed to help us catch explanations that could be clearer. Darrell Feldmar, who came into the project in the final days, gave us her perspective as a typical user and helped us fine tune copy for the book cover.

- Our User Review Team offered helpful opinions and reactions during a two-week "test drive" before final publication. Myrna Blenner, Mark Callahan, David Ensel, Lois Ensel, Kevin McDonald, Christy Morgan and Scott Utzinger let me know what I still needed to clarify. Since their opinions represent areas as diverse as audit, human resources, law, systems, retail, manufacturing and marketing, they gave me a valid measure of the book's clarity and user-friendly style.

- The Business Style Guide would have been impossible, of course, without the thousands of workshop participants who asked the questions that formed the basis of this book. Their honesty helped me to recognize what's really important to them, and their appreciation continued to motivate me to give this project my best efforts.

Joy Van Skiver
Chatham, New Jersey

Contents

Business Style Guide

a lot 1

Abbreviations 1
   Abbreviations to Avoid 1
   Accepted Abbreviations 2
   Punctuation and Spacing 2
   Plurals 2
   Possessives 3
   Abbreviating States 3
   Latin Abbreviations 4
   Two Forms for the Same Term 4

accept/except 5

Acronyms 6
   Creating Acronyms 7
   Using an Acronym the First Time 7
   Possessives 8
   Plurals 8
   When to Use *A* or *An* 9
   Special Note 10

Active Voice/Passive Voice 11
   Understanding Active and Passive 11
   Recognizing Active and Passive 11
   Assigning Responsibility 12
   Why Active Voice is Better Style 13
   How to Change from Passive to Active 15
   Tense vs. Voice 18
   Mixing Active and Passive 18
   Active Directions and Procedures 18
   Active Recommendations 19

advice/advise 20

affect/effect 21
   Other Key Words 21
   In/Into Effect 22
   Effective/Affective 22
   Effect as a Verb 22

all ready/already 23

all right 23

among/between 23

amount/number 24

anxious/eager 25

Apostrophe 26
   When and How to Use the Possessive Form 26
   When You Don't Need Apostrophes 26
   Plural and Possessive 27
   How the "of Test" Helps 28
   Notice of Hours, Days or Weeks 28
   Words Ending in s or z 29
   Joint Possession 29
   Contractions 30
   Uncommon Situations Requiring Apostrophes 30

as well as 31
   Commas 31
   Subject-Verb Agreement 32
   Why Not Use And? 32

assure/ensure/insure 33

Attention Lines 35

because 35
   Commas 36
   The Reason is Because 36

being that 37

bi/semi 37
   Biannual 37
   Hyphens 37

board 38
   Singular or Plural? 38
   Capitalizing 38

cannot 38

Capitalization 39
   Departments, Programs, Projects and Places 39
   Personal Titles 42
   Locations 43
   Seasons 43
   Publications 43
   All Capitals 44
   Shortened Forms 44

Contents

cc 45
   Alphabetical Order 45
   Top or Bottom 45
   Blind Carbon Copies 45

Colon 46

Comma 47
   Too Many Commas 47
   Reasons for Commas 47
   Qualifying Starters 47
   Qualifying Endings 48
   Contrast or Transition 49
   Interrupters 49
   Restrictive Expressions 50
   Items in a Series 50
   Time or Place Phrases 52
   And, *But*, and *Or* with Two Complete Thoughts 53
   And, *But*, and *Or* with Two Verbs 53

Complimentary Closings 54
   How to Choose the Right Closing 54
   Capitalizing, Punctuating and Spacing 54
   Letters Only 55
   International Memos 55
   Declining Formality? 55

complimentary/complementary 56

Contractions 57
   Determining the Limits of Informality 57
   Typical Contractions 57
   Negatives 57
   Technical Writing 58

Dash 59
   Choosing Commas or Colons Instead 59
   Dramatic Emphasis 60
   Not Two Hyphens 60
   Em or En Dash 60
   Spacing 61

Dates 62
   Commas 62
   Year Too? 63
   st, *nd*, *rd* and *th* 63
   Abbreviations 63
   Slashes 64

Military Style or International Style 64
Decades 64
Centuries 64

different from/different than 65
From – The Safer Choice 65
From What 65
Than 66

E-Mail 66
Stream of Consciousness 66
Formatting 66
Stop Shouting 67
Are Typos Acceptable? 67
When to Use E-mail Plus a Memo 67
Beware of Flaming 67
Salutations and Closings 68
Reference Lines 68

Ellipsis 69

Ethnic Groups, Races and Nationalities 70

Exclamation Point 71

farther/further 72
Additional or *More* 72
To a Greater Extent 72
Actual Distance 72

fewer/less 73

Fonts 74
Understanding Fonts 74
Using Fonts Effectively 74
Spacing Between Sentences 74
Type Size 75
What to Avoid 75
Related References 75

formally/formerly 76

Fragments 77

graduated/was graduated 77

have/has/had 78
I Have Enclosed 78
How Tense Affects Meaning 79
Switching Tenses 80
Two Common Mistakes 80
Errors in Speaking 81

… have/ … of 82

Contents

he/she/him/her 82
    Take Out the Word I 82
    Subjects vs. Objects 83
    Caution with *Before*, *After* and *Than* 83
    Avoiding Sexist Writing 84

Headings 84
    Minimum Requirement: Two 84
    No Underlines 84
    Letters and Numbers 85
    specific, Not General 85
    Typefaces 85
    All Caps 85

hopefully 86

however 87

Hyphenated Words 88
    Form Follows Function 88
    Compound Adjectives After a Noun 89
    Mid 90
    Re 90
    Non 90
    Multi 91
    Numbers 91
    Financial Terms 91
    Words with *ly* 91
    Miscellaneous Terms 92
    Word Division 92

i.e. and e.g. 93

imply/infer 93

Italics 94
    Titles 94
    Words Singled Out 94
    Extra Emphasis 94
    Mechanical Details 94

its/it's 95
    Why People Get Confused 95
    Mental Trick to Remember 96

lend/loan 96

Letters 97
    Standard Styles 97
    Typing vs. Word Processing 98
    Date Line 98

Internet in an Hour Business Communication and E-mail   v

Inside Address 98
  Vertical Spacing 99
  Margins 99
  More than One Page 99
  Related References 103
  Examples in This Chapter 103

Lists **104**
  Parallel Structure 104
  Bullets 104
  Alignment 105
  Upper or Lower Case 105
  Punctuation 105
  When to List 106
  White Space 106

me/myself/I **107**

Memos **108**
  Required Items 108
  Optional Items 108
  Personalized Openings 108
  Alignment 109
  Related References 109

Modifying Phrases **111**
  Where to Look for Mistakes 111
  Problems with *ing* and *ed* Endings 112
  Other Problem Phrases 113

none **114**

Numbers **115**
  Spelling Out Numbers 115
  Dollars and Percents 115
  Mixing Figures and Words 116
  st, *nd*, *rd* or *th* 118
  Hyphenating Compound Numbers 118
  Using Parentheses 119
  Readability of Numbers in Text 119
  More Information 119

Open Punctuation **120**

Paragraphs **120**
  Ten Line Maximum 120
  Variety 120
  Breathing Space 120
  One Liners 121
  Indenting 121
  White Space 121

Contents

Parallelism **123**
   Parallel Sentences 123
   Parallel Lists 124

Parentheses **126**
   Problems with Parentheses 126
   Punctuation with Parentheses.. 127

Prepositions **128**

principal/principle **129**

Pronouns **130**
   Rules for Agreement 130
   Missing Antecedents 130
   Avoiding Sexist Writing.. 131
   Clarifying Antecedents 132
   Possessive Pronouns.. 132
   More Information 132

quicker/quickly **133**

Quotation Marks **134**
   Someone's Exact Words 134
   Special Interpretations 135
   No Quotes Necessary... 135
   Commas and Periods... 135
   Rules You Rarely Need... 136

Reference/Subject Lines **137**
   Are Reference Lines
     Required? 137
   Placement and Format.. 137
   Content 138
   E-Mail... 139
   Two Lines: Reference and Subject 139

Run-on Sentences **140**
   Two Sentences, Not One 140
   However, *Therefore* and *Also* 141
   Changing Relationships 141
   Semicolons, or *And* and *But* 142

Salutations **143**
   First Name Only 143
   Initials but No First Name.. 143
   Distinguishing Male and Female Names........................ 143
   No Name Given... 144
   Ms., *Mrs.* or *Miss* 145
   Dr. 146
   Esq. 146

Semicolon **147**
   Horizontal Lists 147
   Misuse of Semicolons 147

Sentence Length **148**
   Balancing Short and Long 148
   Limiting Short Sentences 148

Split Infinitives **149**

Subject-Verb Agreement **150**
   Prepositional Phrases 150
   There 151
   Enclosed and *The Following* 152
   Is, *Are*, *Was*, *Were*, *Has* and *Have* 152
   Anyone, *Each*, *One* and *Everyone* 153
   Two Subjects, One Verb 154
   Or and *Nor* 155
   As Well As, *But Not* and Other Interrupters 155
   Team, *Committee* and *Group* 156
   Data 156
   Number and *Variety* 157
   Total 157
   None 158
   Two Verbs, One Subject 158
   Subordinate Clauses 158

supposed to **160**

than/then **160**

that/which **161**
   Tests to Determine *That* or *Which* 162
   Cutting *That* 163
   Which Hunting 163

the reason being **164**

used to **165**

who/whom **165**

whose/who's **166**

you/your with ing Words **167**

your/you're **168**
   Substitution Test 168
   Why Apostrophes Cause Confusion 169

Business Judgement:
Simple Steps to E-mail Success

Privacy 171
Liability 172
E-mail Overhead 173
Response Time 174
Proactive Communication 174
Just the Facts 175

Using E-Mail Software

Netscape Messenger: 1 178
Netscape Messenger: 2 185
Netscape Messenger: 3 192
Outlook Express: 4 195
Outlook Express: 5 205
Outlook Express: 6 215
America Online E-mail: 7 219
America Online E-mail: 8 223
America Online E-mail: 9 226

Index 227

x

Business Style Guide
Terms for Business Use

a lot

The only correct way to spell *a lot* is to use one word for *a* and another one for *lot*. *Alot* is incorrect.

> We have received a lot of requests for a simplified form.

To help you remember what is correct, imagine some ridiculous comparisons. Can you picture the confusion if people started using *afew, acouple,* or *alittle?*

Abbreviations

People often confuse abbreviations with acronyms. Since most abbreviations use periods but acronyms do not, the styles you need for them are different. An abbreviation is a shortened form of a word or phrase used to represent the full form. For example, *Mon.* is an abbreviation of *Monday.*

An acronym is a word formed by combining initial letters or syllables of two or more words. *ESOP*, for example, is an acronym for *Employee Stock Ownership Plan.* Refer to pages 6 through 10 for rules about creating and using acronyms.

Abbreviations to Avoid

Avoid abbreviating months and days of the week in the text of your correspondence. While abbreviations may be necessary in charts or graphs because of limited space, they tend to give the text of your document a less polished appearance.

Decide what's appropriate based on your document and your audience. If you're writing a letter to a customer, for example, you want the most polished look possible.

> When we meet on Tuesday, October 12, we can clarify our goals for the project.

>> That sentence has a more polished look than one with abbreviations: When we meet on Tues., Oct. 12, we can clarify our goals for the project.

Abbreviations

Accepted Abbreviations

You need to use abbreviations for:

- Terms that you never see spelled out, such as *A.M.*, *P.M.* and *etc*.

    Andrew has scheduled the staff meeting for 8:00 A.M.

    > The standard style for *A.M.* and *P.M.* is to use either lower case or characters known as small caps. If you cannot use small caps on your word processor, choose lower case.

- Professional and academic degrees, such as *M.B.A.*, *Ph.D.*, *B.A.* and *B.S.*

    LaChonne is going to the Wharton School in Philadelphia for her M.B.A.

    > The full name of the degree, *Master of Business Administration*, is rarely used except on certificates.

- Terms accepted as abbreviations in your business, such as *s.k.u.*, *B.T.U.* and *C.O.D.*

    Do you have the s.k.u. number for this product?

    > No one uses the term *stock keeping unit*; everyone in manufacturing and retail knows that items have s.k.u. numbers.

    We expect to ship your order C.O.D.

    > The words *collect on delivery* are seldom written out.

Punctuation and Spacing

Remember two simple rules: no space after each period and no extra period at the end of a sentence.

Plurals

Use an apostrophe and *s* to form the plural of an abbreviation. Since you do not use apostrophes to form plurals of words or acronyms, there is room for confusion here. Just remember that abbreviations are different because they have periods.

> **We stocked two sizes and therefore had two s.k.u.'s for this product in December.**
>
> **Seven C.P.A.'s applied for the position.**
>
> **Is that air conditioner rated at 20,000 B.T.U.'s?**
>
> **We considered candidates with M.B.A.'s or Ph.D.'s.**

Business Style Guide

Abbreviations

Possessives

Use the possessive form of an abbreviation only if you are confident that your reader will not confuse it with the plural form. Since you must use an apostrophe and *s* to form both the plural and the possessive, it is safer to rewrite the sentence than to risk being misunderstood. This is especially important in a paragraph or section of a document where you need to use both plurals and possessives.

> The C.P.A. with four years of experience in a Big Six firm will have an edge as she competes for the new position in Corporate Accounting. Traditionally, C.P.A.'s from Big Six firms have impressed our Vice President of Finance.
>
> Those two sentences are clear.
>
> The C.P.A.'s four years of experience in a Big Six firm will give her an edge as she competes for the new position in Corporate Accounting. Traditionally, C.P.A.'s from Big Six firms have impressed our Vice President of Finance.
>
> Sentences that have both the plural and possessive forms may cause your readers to stop and focus on the abbreviations rather than on your message.

Abbreviating States

Spell out the names of states in business text. The two-letter postal abbreviations without periods are acceptable in addresses, in lists of three or more states, and in charts or tables. For the District of Columbia, always use *DC* without periods.

> Ms. Gomez relocated from our Washington, DC office to the operations center in Weehawken, New Jersey.
>
> The improving economy has enabled us to increase staff significantly at our branches in Reading, Pennsylvania and Newark, Delaware.
>
> The Northeastern Sales Region has offices in Andover, MA; Fairfield, CT; Washington, DC and Wayne, NJ.

Since the traditional abbreviations for states (*Ariz.*, *Calif.*, *Conn.*, *Ill.*, *Mass.*, *Minn.*, *Miss.*, *Penna.*, *Wash.*, etc.) are becoming less common, use them only if this is an established style in your organization.

3

Abbreviations

Latin Abbreviations

Limit your use of the Latin abbreviations *i.e.* and *e.g.* to items given in parentheses, and make sure you use them correctly. The meaning of *i.e.* is "that is"; *e.g.* means "for example." Neither one means "such as." If you use *i.e.* or *e.g.*, place a comma after the abbreviation.

> The program will help our organizations work together in a range of key ways (e.g., integrating training resources, providing job opportunities and developing career-building programs).

Another choice is to eliminate the Latin abbreviations.

> The program will help our organizations work together in a range of key ways. For example, we can integrate training resources, provide job opportunities and develop career-building programs.

Refer to page 120 for more information about *i.e.* and *e.g.*

Two Forms for the Same Term

Have you noticed that some abbreviations use upper case and others use lower case? (*C.O.D.* and *c.o.d.* are both correct.) You may also see some standard business terms used with periods or without periods. While it is correct to use *s.k.u.*, for example, it is also correct to use *SKU*. If you do not use periods, follow the rules for acronyms (pages 6 through 10), not abbreviations.

> We stocked two sizes and therefore had two SKUs for this product in December.
>> There's no need for an apostrophe as in the *s.k.u.* example on page 2 because there are no periods. This form uses the rules for acronyms.

accept/except

To distinguish these two words, remember that *ex* means "not." (The ex-mayor is not the mayor. An *X* is used to cross things out or to *ex*clude them.) The word *except* means "not including."

> Everyone in the department except Cynthia will attend the conference.
>
> We have received all the reports except one.
>
> The processing of orders has improved significantly in the last six months except for a few minor delays.

The word *accept* means "take what someone offers."

> When you accept someone's resignation, you may experience a sense of failure.
>
> We have been accepting more returns due to defects in the binding.
>
> Inez accepted the new position on Thursday.

Be careful if your sentence has the word *not* in it. Since the *ex* in *except* already means "not," you probably want *accept* after *not*.

> She does not accept phone interruptions on Mondays.
>
> We do not accept checks.
>
> We cannot accept parts that have not passed our stringent quality standards.

There is no word *exceptable*. If you're choosing a word that sounds like it, you definitely want *acceptable*.

> We accept any form of payment except checks. Credit cards and traveler's checks are both acceptable.

There is no word *acception*. If you're choosing a word that sounds like it, you definitely want *exception*.

> The only exception to our standard procedure is to use overnight mail when the request comes from a client.

Acronyms

Acronyms help you avoid repeating lengthy names of organizations or departments, or standard terminology within a field. They are essentially new words formed from the first letters of key words. The standard form is to use all upper case and no periods.

Most acronyms are pronounced as words, but some are pronounced letter by letter.

> Most technical professionals know the Occupational Safety and Health Administration as OSHA.
>
> *OSHA* is pronounced just the way it looks: *O shah*.
>
> A major concern about the North American Free Trade Agreement (NAFTA) is the impact on unemployment. Supporters believe NAFTA's impact will be positive.
>
> *NAFTA* is pronounced as a word: *NAF tah*.
>
> He has worked at Quality Value Services (QVS) for six years and expects to be part of QVS's senior management team within the next two years.
>
> *QVS* is pronounced as separate letters: *kew vee ess*.
>
> If there are problems, you will need to contact the SEC.
>
> *SEC* is pronounced as separate letters: *ess ee see*. For people in the financial world, the Securities and Exchange Commission is so well known that it is unnecessary to define the term.
>
> All of our audit reports are prepared according to generally accepted accounting principles (GAAP).
>
> *GAAP* is pronounced as a word: *gap*.
>
> The Financial Accounting Standards Board (FASB) issued new guidelines in August for reporting on a statutory basis. FASB will clarify the procedures in a statement this month.
>
> *FASB* is pronounced as a word: *FAZ be*.

After years of exposure, acronyms sometimes become words with upper and lower case or all lower case. When this happens, it's easy to forget what the letters stand for.

> The stock is listed with Nasdaq.
>
> People rarely use the term *National Association of Security Dealers Automated Quotations*.

Acronyms

> Radar detectors have gained popularity in the last decade.
>> Did you know *radar* stands for the words *radio detecting and ranging*?
>
> We need a sku for the new product ClearLens.
>> Note that the word *sku* is pronounced *skew*. The words *stock keeping unit* would seem unnatural to anyone who works in a retail environment.

Creating Acronyms

When you need to repeat the name of a department or a reference to standard terminology, you can create an acronym. The words you are referring to may or may not begin with upper case.

> Managers in Internal Financial Reporting (IFR) will meet next week to determine IFR's staffing needs for the next two years.
>
> Almost every corporation has an employee-assistance program (EAP). Not only are these programs valuable for all employees, but EAPs also help curb the use of a company's medical benefits.
>
> If you plan to participate in our employee stock ownership plan (ESOP), return the enclosed ESOP form by March 15.
>
> The new research project on Pandymonium Substrate Technology (PST) is proceeding as we expected. We plan to complete the PST project by October.

Using an Acronym the First Time

Unless the acronym is well known by everyone you are writing to, write out the whole term followed by the acronym in parentheses the first time you use it.

> At a recent meeting of the International Computer Association (ICA), experts in the field speculated that a merger of the two giants would have a major impact on price controls in the industry. ICA expects to keep a close watch on this development.

Readers who are familiar with the acronym will not be bothered by the extra words because they will skim right over them. Readers who are not familiar with the acronym will understand your message immediately without pausing to question an unknown word. For all other references in the same document, use the acronym alone without parentheses.

Acronyms

Installing a local area network (LAN) will permit desk-to-desk networking among database users and will free up the mainframe by allowing for greater PC storage. Using a LAN is the most feasible way to upgrade the system without incurring the costs of a major hardware purchase.

Possessives

Use an apostrophe and *s* to create the possessive form, just as you do for most words. You can test the need for a possessive by turning the words around and including the word *of*.

> We have awarded a contract to the Clarkstown Recycling Center (CRC) to handle our paper, glass, plastic and aluminum recyclables. CRC's reputation for not disrupting the workplace is excellent.
>
> The reputation of CRC is excellent.
>
> OSHA's requirements concern safety and health standards nationwide.
>
> The requirements of OSHA concern safety and health standards nationwide.
>
> AMA's goal is to play an active role in health care reform.
>
> The goal of the AMA is to play an active role in health care reform.

Plurals

When you need to form the plural of an acronym, use only an *s*, not an apostrophe and *s*. Remember that acronyms are just like words.

> Of the 17 PCs in our department, only 4 use the latest version of the operating system.
>
> If you were using words instead of the acronym, you would refer to *17 personal computers*.
>
> If you are a corporate business manager (CBM), you will need to set aside several hours a week for phone contact. Most of the CBMs on our staff find they need a minimum of three hours a day to talk with clients on the phone.
>
> If you were using words instead of the acronym, you would refer to *corporate business managers*.
>
> Five CRTs need to be replaced this year.
>
> If you were using words instead of the acronym, you would refer to *cathode ray tubes*.

Business Style Guide

Acronyms

When to Use A or An

Decide on these articles based on the sound, not the letter, that follows. If an acronym begins with a vowel sound, use *an*. If it begins with a consonant sound, use *a*. For acronyms pronounced as words, you probably don't need to think about choosing *a* or *an* because your ear gives you the right answer.

When an acronym is pronounced as a series of letters, however, watch out for the starting letters *f, h, l, m, n, r* and *s*. Although these letters are consonants, they are pronounced as vowel sounds.

> Color is an extremely important factor to consider in the design of an FSI.
>> *FSI*, which stands for *Free Standing Insert*, begins with the sound *ef*.
>
> My company replaced its self-insured plan with an HMO.
>> *HMO*, which stands for *health maintenance organization*, begins with the sound *aitch*.
>
> Based on his experience in other companies, my manager has very strong opinions about reorganizing after an LBO.
>> *LBO*, which stands for *leveraged buyout*, begins with the sound *el*.
>
> This department has initiated an MBO approach.
>> *MBO*, which stands for *management by objectives*, begins with the sound *em*.
>
> One of our community relations meetings featured an NRA lobbyist.
>> *NRA*, which stands for *National Rifle Association*, begins with the sound *en*.
>
> Before we can proceed with a more specific plan, we need to prepare an RFP.
>> *RFP*, which stands for *Request for Proposal*, begins with the sound *ar*.
>
> When she was with the SEC, she spent weeks investigating and unraveling multimillion dollar questions.
>> *SEC*, which stands for *Securities and Exchange Commission*, begins with the sound *ess*.

Acronyms pronounced as letters and starting with the vowels *a, e, i*, and *o* use *an*. However, the vowel *u* often begins acronyms that are pronounced as the consonant *y* sound.

Acronyms

> New marketing decisions were announced last week by an IBM executive.
>> *IBM*, which stands for *International Business Machines*, begins with the sound *eye*.
>
> Using a UPC has simplified our tracking process.
>> *UPC*, which stands for *Universal Product Code*, begins with the sound *yoo*.

Always decide based on sound. Remember that the actual words may require *a* while the acronym requires *an*, or vice versa.

> More than 20 supervisors have asked to participate in a management by objectives (MBO) meeting this quarter. If you are already scheduled to participate in an MBO meeting, please confirm the dates with the General Manager's office before Friday.
>
> Because I lost computer data during the recent power failure, I've decided to buy an uninterruptible power supply (UPS). Many computer users, I learned the hard way, would not be without a UPS.

Special Note

To keep the rules simple for you, we have chosen to define any shortened form without periods as an acronym. Other sources may give you the same rules but refer to abbreviations with periods and abbreviations without periods.

Most business professionals need to use the style clearly established for acronyms. If your organization uses a style with periods, follow the rules given for abbreviations on pages 1 through 4.

You may also notice differences in style in standard publications such as *The New York Times* and *The Wall Street Journal*. For example, the *Times* uses *I.B.M.* while the *Journal* uses *IBM*. Keep in mind that newspapers and other publications have specific style guides that their writers must adhere to for consistency within the publications.

Business Style Guide

Active Voice/Passive Voice

Both active voice and passive voice are grammatically correct. However, active voice is usually clearer and therefore your better choice for business.

If you are using a grammar checker on a personal computer, it may tell you that you have used passive voice. Or, your manager may tell you that you use too much passive voice. To decide what is appropriate for your documents, you need to understand both active and passive voice and know why active voice is usually better.

Every time you speak or write, you use either active or passive voice in verb forms. Since most people speak in active voice, it's easier and more natural to write in the same style.

Understanding Active and Passive

Passive voice always has two parts: a form of *be* (*is, are, was, were, be, being, been*) and a main verb that ends in *ed, d, en* or *t*.

> The strategy that has been suggested includes an increase in direct mail marketing.
>> *Has been suggested* is passive voice. Although there is nothing grammatically wrong with that sentence, the use of passive voice may have an impact on the reader's understanding. The person or people who suggested the strategy may influence someone's decision to implement or not to implement the strategy. Using passive voice in the sentence makes it possible to leave out who did the suggesting.

> Alicia, our marketing research consultant, suggested a new strategy that includes an increase in direct mail marketing.
>> *Suggested* is active voice; it forces the writer to identify who did the suggesting. Alicia may add considerable credibility because her area of expertise is market research. However, if Alicia's suggestions in the past have not been home runs, the decision maker may not value the advice.

Recognizing Active and Passive

Active voice may have a verb form that ends in *ed, d, en* or *t*, but it will not have a form of *be* (*is, are, was, were, be, being, been*) along with that verb.

> Extra measures should be implemented to ensure that the new plant produces flawless materials.
>> *Should be implemented* is a verb form in passive voice. Note the word *be* and the *ed* ending in the word *implemented*.

11

Active Voice/Passive Voice

Hans, the plant manager, has implemented extra measures to ensure that the new plant produces flawless materials.

> *Has implemented* is a verb form in active voice. The verb *implemented* ends with an *ed*, but there is no form of the word *be*.

All candidates are carefully screened by Human Resources before they meet with the Director of Personnel.

> *Are carefully screened* is a verb form in passive voice. The word *are* is a form of *be*, and *screened* ends in *ed*. *Meet* is a verb ending in *t*, but since there is no form of *be*, this verb is in active voice.

Human Resources carefully screens all candidates before sending them to meet with the Director of Personnel.

> There is no passive voice in that sentence because there are no forms of the word *be* combined with a verb form ending in *ed, d, en* or *t*.

Marty is the supervisor in charge of Accounts Payable.

> That sentence has a form of the word *be* (*is*), but there is no verb form ending in *ed, d, en* or *t*. Therefore, the sentence is in active voice.

Assigning Responsibility

In business documents, passive voice can cause problems because people do not understand who is responsible for an action. The confusion usually occurs with memos or reports that have large distribution lists. When you are directing a memo or report to Distribution, make sure you use active voice.

The record needs to be revised to reflect current activity on this account.

> *Needs to be revised* is passive voice. Unless other sentences clarify who should do the revising, several people may read the sentence and think someone else is going to revise the record. The risk is that no one will revise the record.

Business Style Guide

Active Voice/Passive Voice

Monthly sales reports should be reviewed once a year to determine the extent of face-to-face customer contact.

Should be reviewed is passive voice. If that sentence is in a memo from a regional sales manager to district sales managers and account managers, will everyone reading it know who is responsible for reviewing the reports?

Account managers should review their monthly sales reports once a year to determine the extent of face-to-face customer contact.

Everyone reading that sentence knows the account managers are responsible; the active voice forces the writer to assign responsibility.

When the reader does not need to know who is doing an action, passive voice is acceptable.

The brochures will be printed early next week.

Will be printed is passive voice. If the reader does not care about the printer, there is no need to identify who is doing the printing.

Why Active Voice is Better Style

Your readers should hear your voice as they are reading. This is especially important in correspondence to clients, in directions and procedures, and in proposals. When you use passive voice, your document may sound stilted, distant, or even condescending.

Active voice helps you to be direct, concise and reader-focused. Note the contrast in a memo written in passive voice on this page and in active voice on pages 14 and 15.

Active Voice/Passive Voice

> The new schedule for insurance seminars has been released by the Customer Relations Department. To give us enough time for processing, all registration forms must be returned to me by the deadlines on the attached list.
>
> Attached is an Insurance Seminar Registration Application. Every box that is "Xed" should be completed. If blank application forms are needed, they can be obtained by contacting Joanne Spencer at extension 3604.
>
> If you have any questions about the courses, I can be reached at extension 4630.

The passive verbs in that memo include:

has been released	*should be completed*
must be returned	*are needed*
Attached is	*can be obtained*
is "Xed"	*can be reached*

Business Style Guide

Active Voice/Passive Voice

> The Customer Relations Department has released the new schedule for insurance seminars. To give us enough time for processing, please return your registration forms by the deadlines on the attached list.
>
> Complete all items marked with an "X" on the application I've attached. If you need more forms, call Joanne Spencer at extension 3604.
>
> If you have any questions about the courses, call me at extension 4630.

The active verbs in that memo include:

has released	*call*
return	*have*
Complete	*call*
need	

How to Change from Passive to Active

There are three primary methods you can use to change passive voice to active.

- Identify who is performing the action and include that information before the verb. Frequently, the word *by* is in a sentence with passive voice. When that is the case, move the words that follow the word *by* to the beginning of the sentence. The verb that fits logically will be in active voice. This "who first" method is one you can use frequently.

   Changes to the current budget reporting system will be implemented by accounting.

   Will be implemented is passive voice.

   Accounting will implement changes to the current budget reporting system.

   Will implement is active voice.

15

Active Voice/Passive Voice

- Use the infinitive form (*to* plus a verb). By choosing a *to do* phrase instead of passive voice, you can change the tone of a sentence from judgmental to diplomatic.

  Factors that should be considered during our reorganization include time management, personnel and training.

  Should be considered is passive voice.

  Factors to consider during our reorganization include time management, personnel and training.

  To consider is active voice.

- Start with an action word. When you want your reader to perform the action, drop the form of *be* and the *ed, d, en* or *t* on the end of the verb. Since this is the most direct of the methods, use it for procedures and other directions.

  The procedure for transferring funds needs to be changed to include the new data.

  Needs to be changed is passive voice.

  Change the procedure for transferring funds to include the new data.

  Change is active voice.

To maintain an acceptable tone and an interesting style, try to use all three methods. Changing to active voice by using only action words first could make your document sound too demanding. Using only the "who first" method could be monotonous.

Active Voice/Passive Voice

The following paragraph is an example of passive voice:

> Enclosed is a set of master copies of the work tickets that have been collected from your company. Rather than writing on these tickets, copies should be made of these masters. It is also recommended that the master copies be customized so that your specific needs are met. After the work tickets have been customized, the master copies should be kept at your printing site.

Here is the same paragraph written primarily in active voice:

> Enclosed is a set of master copies of the work tickets that we collected from your company. Rather than writing on these tickets, make copies of these masters. We also recommend that you customize the master copies to meet your specific needs. After you customize the work tickets, keep the master copies at your printing site.

Active Voice/Passive Voice

Did the second paragraph on page 17 sound more user-friendly to you than the first one? The following columns identify the method used to change each passive verb in the first paragraph to an active verb in the second paragraph:

Passive	Active	Method Used
have been collected	*we collected*	*who* first
should be made	*make*	action first
is also recommended	*we recommend*	*who* first
be customized	*you customize*	*who* first
are met	*to meet*	infinitive
have been customized	*you customize*	*who* first
be kept	*keep*	action first

Tense vs. Voice

If you think you must use passive voice because the action occurred in the past, you may be confusing tense and voice. Tense refers to time; you can remember this by associating the *t* with *tense* and *time*. Voice is always there no matter when the action occurs. Note that all verbs have both voice and tense:

> Hadil, who is in charge of the project, found only one procedure for us to review when we meet next week.
>
> | *is* | active voice, present tense |
> | *found* | active voice, past tense |
> | *meet* | active voice, present tense |
>
> Only one procedure was identified that will be reviewed at our meeting next week.
>
> | *was identified* | passive voice, past tense |
> | *will be reviewed* | passive voice, future tense |

Mixing Active and Passive

It is grammatically correct and often necessary to mix active and passive voice in the same document, even in the same paragraph. If you create technical reports, for example, there may be places where it is inappropriate or illogical to identify who is doing the action.

Active Directions and Procedures

If you have ever struggled to understand directions that were not clear, you can empathize with people who get lost in a muddle of passive instructions.

Business Style Guide

Active Voice/Passive Voice

When you need to write directions or procedures, avoid the two most common passive expressions:

- *must be* plus a verb ending in *ed, d, en* or *t*
- *should be* plus a verb ending in *ed, d, en* or *t*

Since this style often shows up in documents going to several people, think of talking to one person when you write. Choose the same words you would use in person to explain actions that someone must take. You will probably find that you think and speak in active voice.

Can you imagine the chaos all of us would have to deal with if everyone gave travel directions in passive voice?

> New Jersey Route 24 should be taken to Interstate 78. This should be followed until U.S. Route 1 North is reached. The Pulaski Skyway should be taken to the Holland Tunnel.

Active voice is so much easier to understand, and it sounds natural to everyone.

> Take New Jersey Route 24 to Interstate 78. Follow this until you reach U.S. Route 1 North. Take the Pulaski Skyway to the Holland Tunnel.

If it's logical to use active voice when telling someone how to get from one place to another, isn't it logical to use it for business directions?

Active Recommendations

Avoid the expression *it is recommended*. If you're not comfortable identifying who is recommending, try using a heading followed by listed items in active voice.

> Recommendation: Establish new procedures for processing authorized sales orders.
>
> > That typical line from an audit report is much more effective than the following sentence in passive voice: It is recommended that new procedures be established for processing authorized sales orders.

Recommendations
- Install a local area network (LAN) before January 15.
- Initiate training sessions for all PC users.
- Establish a help line with 24-hour support.

19

Active Voice/Passive Voice

> That typical section of a proposal to senior management is much more effective than a series of sentences beginning with: *It is recommended that* .... Each bullet point could also include several lines explaining the benefits of each recommendation.

Introducing a sentence with a qualifying statement can substantiate your position before you make your recommendation. This structure is effective when you want to use *I* or *we*.

> Based on our review of the current procedures, we recommend developing a new Retirement Plan Processing Guide.

> To ensure that increased overhead costs do not affect profit, we recommend raising our rates by 9%.

advice/advise

If you're not sure of the distinction between these two words, recognize that pronunciation is one key to getting them straight. The one that rhymes with *nice* is the noun. (Think of giving someone "nice advice.") The one that rhymes with *wise* is the verb. (Only the "wise" should "advise.")

> My manager gave me some very good advice about getting ahead in this company.

> Has your lawyer advised you of your financial obligation?

Business Style Guide

affect/effect

One way to determine which word you need is to use the "Double E Rule." Test the sentence by putting the article *the* in front of *affect* or *effect*. If the sentence is logical when you read it with *the*, you want the word with the *E*. Think of *thE Effect*.

> The effect of lower interest rates has been positive for our business.
>> If you were thinking of using *affect*, the "Double E Rule" would give you the right answer — *effect*—immediately.
>
> Our department meeting will focus on the effect of recent system changes.
>> If you were thinking of using *affect*, the "Double E Rule" would give you the right answer — *effect*—immediately.

Using the "Double E Rule" helps you because *effect* is a noun. It means "the result of something" or "the reaction to something that was done."

> Our marketing research identified the effect of image on buying decisions.
>
> If we are going to have any effect on the final outcome, we must work together to solve the immediate problems.

The word *affect* means "do something to change." Since it is always a verb, it will never make sense with the word *the* immediately before it.

> The current economy affects our decisions.
>> Since it's not logical to say: The current economy **the** affects our decisions, the "Double E Rule" tells you that you need *affects*.
>
> His work has been affected by the increased responsibilities in our department.
>> It's not logical to say: His work has been **the** affected by the increased responsibilities in our department.

Other Key Words

The words *a, an, any* or *one* can help you choose *effect*. Because these words always describe nouns, *effect* is the only correct choice.

> We are looking for any effect of the training that will cause us to change direction.
>
> A lasting effect of our recent move has been decreased absenteeism.
>
> One effect of upgrading our equipment is a new motivation to try techniques we have not used before.

affect/effect

In/Into Effect

The standard expressions *in effect* or *into effect* always use *effect* because a noun must follow the prepositions *in* or *into*.

> The new price list goes into effect January 1.
>
> Those procedures have been in effect as long as I have been with the company.

Effective/Affective

You will often need to use the word *effective* in business.

> Effective immediately, we will no longer rely on voice mail for urgent messages.
>
> An effective alternative to the first suggestion is to hire an outside consultant.

The word *affective* is rarely used in business since it pertains to feelings or emotions.

> Someone who has a seasonal affective disorder may need more light in the winter to counteract feelings of depression.

Effect as a Verb

You rarely need to use *effect* as a verb in business. When you do, it means "bring about." The word *change* often occurs elsewhere in the sentence with this use of *effect*.

> The new manager effected complete changes in our standard operating procedures.
>
> To effect a change in procedures, we began with a survey of all employees.

all ready/already

When you are choosing between *all ready* and *already*, stop to focus on the meaning. If you want to say everything (all) is ready, you need *all ready*.

>The items are all ready for shipment and will go out today.

>Although we have not purchased the software you requested, we do have the hardware all ready for installation.

If you are talking about something that has occurred, you need *already*.

>Since we already billed you for seven cases instead of six, we will issue a credit for the merchandise you have returned.

>Ryan has already completed the first phase of our sales training program.

all right

Using *alright* instead of *all right* is a common mistake. To remember that *all right* is the only correct form, it may help you to think about the opposite meaning. If something is not all right, it is all wrong. Can you imagine writing *alwrong*?

among/between

Use *between* when you are referring to two entities.

>We will split the responsibility between the Administrative Services staff and the Purchasing Department.

>Just between you and me, they've already made a decision.

Use *among* when you are referring to three or more entities.

>The meeting among representatives from Accounting, Auditing and Payroll will focus on this year's financial goals.

>We will divide the tasks equally among the five people in the department.

To avoid sounding like a person from an earlier century, do not use the word *amongst*.

amount/number

Use *amount* when you are talking about something that is a mass, not separate items. Think of the word *mount* within the word *amount* and imagine a mountain of material.

> The amount of trash left on the sidewalk after the refuse haulers' strike was incredible.
>
> Despite a significant amount of trouble, we were able to reconstruct the course of events leading to the error.
>
> My manager is not aware of the amount of work involved in this project.

Dollars are always amounts.

> I never carry that amount of money with me.
>> You are more likely to say: I never carry that much money with me. The word *much* also suggests a mass of something, not separate bills and coins.

Use *number* for items that can be separated and counted as individual units. Associate the word *number* with counting. If you can count the number of items you are referring to, use *number*, not *amount*.

> A number of stockholders have expressed their dissatisfaction with the changes in management.
>
> The average number of meetings to discuss the status of projects is two per week.
>
> We plan to increase the number of programmers assigned to the project.
>
> The number of outstanding invoices affects our cash flow.
>
> When we revised the form, we received just a small number of complaints from customers.

Refer to page 157 for the difference between *a* number and *the* number in subject–verb agreement.

anxious/eager

These two words have been misused for so many years that a lot of readers will never know the difference.

Are you excited and looking forward to something? Then use *eager*. Are you worried about something that lies ahead? Then use *anxious*.

People who do not realize that these words have different connotations may be conveying a negative view when they really want a positive one. In sales correspondence, for example, it is especially important to project confidence.

> **We are eager to move ahead on this project to meet the deadlines you have established.**
>> The customer reading that sentence will perceive the writer as confident and ready to meet the deadlines.
>
> **My supervisor is anxious to hear the vice president's recent decision.**
>> The use of *anxious* suggests that the supervisor has some fear or concern about the decision.

Remembering the word *anxiety* may help you remember the negative connotation of *anxious*. The slang expression *eager beaver* may help you remember the positive connotation of *eager*.

Apostrophe

You need an apostrophe for two common situations: (1) to form the possessive of a noun, and (2) to create a contraction.

> Joanne's direction has given us the motivation to accomplish the goals we've been discussing for two years.

The use of an apostrophe and *s* shows that the word *Joanne's* is the possessive form of *Joanne*. The word *we've* is a contraction for *we have*.

When and How to Use the Possessive Form

For any noun not ending in *s*, form the possessive by adding an apostrophe and *s*. One way to remember this rule is to think of needing a mark (') and a sound (*s*).

You probably learned that the possessive form shows ownership. That's correct.

> Joshua's status report ....

Joshua owns the status report; it belongs to him.

However, the possessive form does not always mean literally that one item belongs to someone or something. If you are not sure whether you need an apostrophe, use the "*of* test" to help you decide. The following examples illustrate how the "*of* test" works:

> Last month's safety record was normal for this time of year.

If you are not sure whether you need *months* or *month's*, read the sentence as: **The safety record of last month** .... Because that wording makes sense, you realize that you are indicating possession; *month's* is correct.

> We have reached this year's goal by increasing profits 10%.

You realize you need an apostrophe when you test by saying: **We have reached the goal of this year** ....

When You Don't Need Apostrophes

Proofread carefully to catch the common mistake of using apostrophes where they are not needed. Remember that apostrophes do not indicate the plural form of words.

> Several employees' have requested summer hours on Fridays in July and August.

That sentence is not correct. The correct word is *employees*; no apostrophe is necessary to indicate more than one employee.

Business Style Guide

Apostrophe

Oliver asked for a list of department's interested in becoming involved in the volunteer program.
> That sentence is not correct. The correct word is *departments*; no apostrophe is necessary to indicate more than one department.

One of my bosses' suggested that I apply for the position open in Information Technology.
> That sentence is not correct. The correct word is *bosses*; no apostrophe is necessary to indicate more than one boss.

Just like words, acronyms do not need apostrophes to form the plural.

Five DM's are choosing the site for our sales meeting.
> That sentence is not correct. The correct plural form is *DMs*; no apostrophe is necessary to indicate more than one district manager.

You do not need apostrophes for the following possessive pronouns: *hers, his, its, ours, theirs, whose* and *yours*.

His airline tickets arrived this morning; hers should be here this afternoon.

Decades, such as *1990s*, do not need apostrophes to indicate the plural. Page 84 gives you more information about references to decades.

Plural and Possessive

When you need to form the possessive of a word that is plural, separate the steps. First, form the plural. Then, form the possessive.

The consultant's report indicated a need for upgrading our professional image.
> There is one consultant. The apostrophe and *s* give you the possessive form.

The consultants' report indicated a need for upgrading our professional image.
> There is more than one consultant; the *s* immediately after the *t* gives you the plural form. The apostrophe after the *s* gives you the possessive form.

To create the plural form of most words, you need to add an *s* or *es*. In these cases, use only an apostrophe after the *s* to show possession. Since you already have the sound (*s*), all you need is the mark (').

Apostrophe

Five agencies' contracts include a cancellation clause.

The plural of *agency* is *agencies*; adding the apostrophe indicates the possessive form.

The bosses' opinions about adapting to change were similar although their experiences were quite different.

The plural of *boss* is *bosses*; adding the apostrophe at the end of *bosses* gives you the possessive form.

Some words do not form the plural by adding an *s* or *es*. In these cases, add an apostrophe and an *s*.

Companies who market children's clothing by direct mail have experienced significant growth in the last decade.

The plural of *child* is *children*; adding the apostrophe and *s* indicates the possessive form of *children*.

How the "of Test" Helps

If the terms *plural* and *possessive* cause you some confusion, rely on the "*of* test" to determine where to place the apostrophe.

Our company's marketing position is based on quality, not on price.

Test by saying: ... the position of our company. You realize you are referring to one company; the apostrophe must go before the *s*.

Our companies' joint venture reflects the current trend of reducing costs for research and development.

Test by saying: ... the joint venture of our companies. You realize you are referring to two or more companies; the apostrophe must go after the *s*.

Notice of Hours, Days or Weeks

When you refer to a time period followed by the word *notice*, you need an apostrophe.

The management consultant requires 48 hours' notice for cancellation without penalty.

Test by saying: The management consultant requires notice of 48 hours .... You realize the word you are using is *hours*, not *hour*; the apostrophe must go after the *s*.

She handed in her resignation and gave two weeks' notice.

She gave notice of two weeks.

Business Style Guide

Apostrophe

Words Ending in s or z

If a noun already ends in *s*, add only an apostrophe to create the possessive form of the word.

> Ross' perspective is that nothing is impossible.
>
> Ms. Aristedes' plan is to provide mentors for each of the new trainees.
>
> My boss' standards are very high.

If you see a different form with an *s* after the apostrophe, recognize that the writer is adhering to traditional rules based on pronunciation.

> Ross's perspective is that nothing is impossible.
>> People who use this possessive form (*Ross's*) say the added *s* shows that everyone hears an extra syllable when pronouncing the word: *Ross es*. Unfortunately, this approach has caused more confusion than clarity for most people. While it is not wrong to use an extra *s*, it is not necessary.

Words ending in *z* use the rule most other words follow to form the possessive: add an apostrophe and *s*.

> Bob Steinmetz's March 15 memo explains the new tax law for special parking privileges.

Joint Possession

When you need to refer to something owned by more than one person or entity, use an apostrophe only after the last name given.

> **Denisha and Alana's report will summarize the benefits of upgrading our software now rather than later.**
>
> There is one report written by two people.

If you use the word *my* or *your*, you may need to rewrite a sentence to keep it from sounding awkward.

> **The cost justification needs John's or my approval.**
>> That sentence is correct. However, it may cause your reader to stop and concentrate on words that do not sound right. You can avoid having your reader slow down by rewriting the sentence: **The cost justification needs John's approval or mine.**

29

Apostrophe

To clarify that two entities have separate ownership, use an apostrophe and *s* for each entity.

> Victor's and Maya's departments will be responsible for testing the new system.
>
> > There are two separate departments; one is Victor's and the other is Maya's. If these two people were in charge of one department, only one apostrophe and *s* would be necessary: Victor and Maya's department will be responsible for testing the new system.

Contractions

When you use contractions, place the apostrophe where there are missing letters. In business, the most common contractions are *I'll, I'm, it's, I've, we've* and *who's*. Refer to pages 57 through 58 for more about contractions.

> I've enclosed the marketing survey you requested.
>
> > *I've* means *I have*.
>
> Claude is the one who's responsible for tracking the data.
>
> > *Who's* means *who is*.

Uncommon Situations Requiring Apostrophes

Apostrophes indicate the plural of letters and numbers.

> Remember to spell *recommendation* with two *m*'s.
>
> He had three 20's in his wallet.

Use an apostrophe when you omit the first two numbers in a year.

> Our department has ambitious goals for '95.

Since abbreviations (shortened forms with periods) are not considered words, they require apostrophes to indicate more than one. Refer to pages 1 through 4 for more information about abbreviations.

> Five Ph.D.'s joined the research group this month.
>
> The committee will be investigating office space in Manhattan as well as New Jersey.

as well as

Most questions about *as well as* pertain to commas. Mistakes also occur, however, with subject–verb agreement.

Commas

When *as well as* comes close to the subject in a sentence, you need a comma before it and another comma soon (but not immediately) after it. The commas are necessary to show you are using an interrupting phrase between the subject and verb. If you were speaking instead of writing, you would probably change the inflection of your voice for the section surrounded by commas in writing.

> Abdul, as well as Virginia, will be working at the trade show.

> Copies of the contracts, as well as the originals, need to be filed in the same drawer.

When *as well as* does not come between the subject and the verb, commas are optional. Decide based on what seems clearer to you.

> We are holding June 17 and 18, as well as June 27 and 28, for our next sales meeting.

>> The commas surrounding the expression *as well as June 27 and 28* help your reader see two separate possibilities for the sales meeting.

> The revised manual is thorough as well as entertaining for people who are not as familiar with the system.

>> The expression *as well as entertaining* does not need commas. However, it would not be incorrect to use commas after *thorough* and *entertaining*.

> Our original plan called for disaster recovery services at an off-site location, as well as temporary office space for more than 200 people.

>> The comma after *location* helps set apart the rest of the sentence as an afterthought.

No commas are necessary when you use *as well as* before one or two words at the end of a sentence.

as well as

Subject–Verb Agreement

To check your subject–verb agreement, remove the interrupting phrase. Occasionally, you will find a sentence that has a singular subject before *as well as* but a plural word after *as well as*.

> Mileage, as well as expenses for meals, is reimbursable.

>> Although that sentence may sound strange to you, it is correct. *Mileage* is a singular subject and therefore requires *is* as the verb. When you remove the interrupting phrase, the sentence sounds fine: Mileage is reimbursable.

>> Another choice you have is to rewrite the sentence: Mileage and expenses for meals are reimbursable.

Why Not Use And?

Although the meaning of *as well as* is the same as the word *and*, they are not used the same way.

> Thomas was assertive as well as diplomatic in his negotiations with the committee.

>> The word *diplomatic* receives slightly more emphasis than the word *assertive*. If you read the sentence aloud, you will probably hear your voice go up on the word *well*. That does not happen with *and*: Thomas was assertive and diplomatic ....

>> The phrase *as well as* creates a change in the rhythm of the words and therefore alters the meaning of the sentence.

> Our new production schedule, as well as the personnel changes needed to implement it, has been approved by the senior partners.

>> The core of that sentence is that the schedule has been approved. Adding the phrase about the personnel changes is a kind of afterthought. When you construct a sentence in this way, you may be suggesting that a lot of your readers already know that the personnel changes have been approved.

> Our new production schedule and the personnel changes needed to implement it have been approved by the senior partners.

>> The core of that sentence is that the schedule and the personnel changes have been approved. Since no afterthought is expressed, the entire sentence is probably new information for everyone reading it.

Business Style Guide

assure/ensure/insure

Although all three of these words are similar, they have separate connotations that may be important for you to recognize. Knowing the shades of difference will help you choose the word that fits the meaning you want.

Insure

The word *insure* is the most familiar of the three. It means "guarantee against risk or loss." This is the only word to use when you know that money is involved in the guarantee. Remember that your *in*surance company is bound by contract to guarantee against loss or risk.

> Since we have just made major hardware purchases, we need to insure this equipment.
>> If the hardware is destroyed in the next flood, the insurance company will provide a payment that allows us to replace the equipment.
>
> Are you planning to insure the new art work?
>> If there is a fire in the building and the art work is ruined, the insurance company will provide a payment that allows us to purchase new art work.

Ensure

The word *ensure* means "make certain." This is the word you want when you are very certain but there could be factors beyond your control.

> I have checked with the shipping department to ensure that you receive your order before March 1.
>> No money was involved. I have done all I can to make sure you receive the order, but the shipping department or the shipper could make a mistake.
>
> We will do everything we can to ensure your satisfaction.
>> Something could happen that would cause you to be dissatisfied.
>
> To ensure that you receive your next delivery on time, I have asked Raymond to double check the order one week before shipment.
>> I have done my part, but will others do theirs?
>
> We have ensured complete data recovery by installing a new backup system.
>> The use of *ensure* allows for the possibility of the new backup system not working at some point. If you want to convey a guarantee that there will be no problems, use the word *insure*.

33

assure/ensure/insure

Assure

The word *assure* means "give confidence or encouragement." Since the word *reassure* is commonly used to refer to an emotional boost, it may help to associate that with *assure*. There is no guarantee here, just a pep talk.

> The flight attendant assured us that the flight would be leaving in 15 minutes.
>> The attendant's assurance is far from a guarantee; even the pilot is not certain until immediately before takeoff.
>
> New hires often need to be assured that they are contributing to productivity.
>> There is no certainty that new hires do contribute to productivity, but some encouragement may help them get past the learning stage, especially if they are taking a lot of someone else's time.
>
> Before I walked up to the podium, my manager assured me that my presentation would be great.
>> The manager's pep talk may be just what I need to boost my confidence.

Business Style Guide

Attention Lines

Attention lines used to be common in business letters. Secretaries typed the word *Attention* followed by a colon and the reader's name on a separate line below the inside address.

Unless you work in a legal area where this style is considered standard, you do not need attention lines. Instead, place the person's name as the first line of the inside address.

> Mr. Louis Alexander
> Chapin and Chapin Associates
> One Corporate Boulevard
> Parsippany, NJ 07054
>
> Dear Mr. Alexander:

because

Yes, it is acceptable to start a sentence with the word *because*. As long as you create a complete sentence, starting with *because* is fine.

> Because we increased the staff in Information Technology, we need to find additional office space that can accommodate special wiring requirements.
>> That sentence is complete because it has a subject and verb and expresses a complete thought: **We need to find additional office space.**

If you remember learning a different rule in elementary school, consider why teachers said you should never start a sentence with *because*. Because second graders are still mastering the concept of complete sentences, it is quite helpful for teachers to discourage sentence fragments such as the following:

> Because I want to.
> Because she said so.
> Because they didn't have enough money.

because

Commas

The word *because* introduces a group of words that cannot stand alone. This group of words is called a subordinate clause. Use a comma after the entire clause when you start a sentence with *because*.

> Because he did not agree with the new CEO's management style, Ed decided to resign.
>> The subordinate clause that cannot stand alone is *Because he did not agree with the new CEO's management style*. The sentence is complete because there is also a main clause that can stand alone: *Ed decided to resign*.

You do not need a comma when you place the subordinate clause at the end of the sentence.

> Ed decided to resign because he did not agree with the new CEO's management style.

The Reason is Because

Using the word *reason* with the word *because* is redundant. Therefore, avoid the construction *the reason is because*. Usually, you can be more direct by changing the sentence.

> There is a backlog in Accounting because we have three people doing the work that used to be done by four.
>> That sentence is much better than: The reason for the backlog in Accounting is because we have three people doing the work that used to be done by four.

> The reason for the backlog in Accounting is that we have three people doing the work that used to be done by four.
>> Substituting the word *that* for *because* is another way to avoid the expression *the reason is because*.

being that

Although you may hear or see the expression *being that*, it is incorrect. The word *since* is a much better choice.

> Since you have 14 interested staff members, I recommend splitting the group in half.
>> That sentence is much better than this one: Being that you have 14 interested staff members, I recommend splitting the group in half.

Refer to page 164 for advice about a similar phrase: *the reason being*.

---

bi/semi

Since it's easy to confuse these two prefixes, you may want to avoid them entirely. If your reader doesn't think they mean what you think they mean, you're leaving yourself open to problems. In a memo, for example, it may be just as convenient to say *twice a week, every two weeks, twice a month, every two months, twice a year,* or *every two years*.

Bi

Think *two* when you see this prefix. It may help to remember that a bicycle has two wheels and that someone who is bilingual speaks two languages.

> *biweekly* — every two weeks
> *bimonthly* — every two months
> *biennial* — every two years

Semi

Think *half* when you see this prefix. If you remember that a semicircle is half a circle, the following words may not be troublesome:

> *semiweekly* — twice a week (half a week)
> *semimonthly* — twice a month (half a month)
> *semiannually* — twice a year (half a year)

Biannual

Avoid using *biannual*, which means "twice a year," not "every two years." Use *semiannual* or the words *every two years* instead.

Hyphens

You do not need hyphens for any word using either of these prefixes.

board

Because this word is not one that most people use every day, there are often questions about agreement with verbs and the use of upper or lower case.

Singular or Plural?

A board always consists of several people; however, the word *board* is always singular. This is American style, not British style.

> The Board of Directors is meeting next week before the annual meeting with stockholders.

The verb *is meeting* agrees with *Board*.

Capitalizing

When you capitalize references to a board, you indicate that the board is part of your own organization. When you use lower case, you indicate that the board is not part of your own organization.

> The Board has accepted our proposal to eliminate unnecessary paperwork.

Because *Board* is capitalized, the reader knows it is his or her own organization's board.

> Kianna has just been selected to become a member of the board of directors at White and Crown, Inc.

Since *board of directors* is in lower case, the reader knows the writer is not part of White and Crown.

---

cannot

Use one word (*cannot*), not two (*can not*). The word *can* is the only word, however, that you can combine with *not* as one word.

> The packaging cannot include the term Fat Free due to recent FDA regulations.

Business Style Guide

Capitalization

When you capitalize words, you give them special emphasis. While there are specific rules to help you decide when to capitalize, you will often have to make a subjective judgment.

When in doubt, undercapitalize. Here's why: You want your readers to pay attention to words, not letters. If you capitalize words that don't need to be capitalized, your readers may shift their attention away from your message as they wonder why you used capital letters.

The following example taken from the Declaration of Independence was standard style in the 18th century, but it may cause you to pause as you notice words that you would not normally capitalize:

> When in the Course of human Events, it becomes necessary for one People to dissolve the political Bonds which have connected them with another, and to assume among the Powers of the Earth, the separate and equal Station to which the Laws of Nature and of Nature's God entitle them, a decent Respect to the Opinions of Mankind requires that they should declare the Causes which impel them to the Separation.

If Thomas Jefferson were writing a similar document at the end of the 20th century, he undoubtedly would eliminate a lot of the capital letters he used in the Declaration of Independence.

Keep in mind as you review the rules that you need to have a good reason for capitalizing. If you don't have one, you can probably use lower case.

Departments, Programs, Projects and Places

Capitalize the first letter of words that name specific departments, special programs or projects, and specific places. Usually you will capitalize specific departmental names within your own organization. By doing so, you indicate that you are an insider and that this unit is significant within the hierarchy of your organization.

Capitalization

The following examples will help you distinguish between terms that need to be capitalized and those that do not.

The Human Resources Department conducts an annual survey to determine how many contracts we have finalized with women-owned businesses.

> By capitalizing *Human Resources Department*, you indicate one specific department.

Unified Electronics has recently initiated a program in Total Quality Management (TQM).

> Since *Total Quality Management* is a specific program, it needs capital letters.

Have you called Accounts Payable to find out why the check is late?

> The name of the department functions in the same way that a person's name would: **Have you called Edna Tyler ...?** Recognizing that distinction is a good way to decide whether or not you need to capitalize a departmental name.

After Joe logs in the checks, he gives them to Mary Jane, a clerk in Accounts Receivable.

> Because *Accounts Receivable* is a specific department in Mary Jane's organization, it is capitalized.

Experience in accounts payable often results in opportunities for career growth.

> By not capitalizing *accounts payable*, you suggest the department could be in any organization.

Give the Customer More in '94 has already had an impact on our customer service agents. This campaign may make a huge difference in the customer survey results at the end of the year.

> By capitalizing *Give the Customer More in '94*, you highlight it as a special project or program.

The Finance Department's training team will meet in Conference Room C on the third floor.

> By capitalizing *Finance Department*, you suggest a specific department within your organization. By not capitalizing *training team*, you suggest that other departments also have training teams.
>
> Since the conference room has a specific name, it needs capital letters.

Business Style Guide

Capitalization

The Musical Arts Foundation cannot give us more information until its finance department reviews next year's budget.

> By not capitalizing *finance department*, you indicate it is one of many finance departments.

The Work Alternatives Committee will meet in the third floor conference room.

> The capitalized words indicate a specific name of the committee. There is no need to capitalize conference rooms designated by specific floors.

Our meeting on Monday will be in the Roundtable Room.

> *Roundtable Room* is a specific name given to a room and therefore needs to be capitalized.

Representatives from our regional offices will be attending the national convention.

> There is no need to capitalize *regional offices* or *national convention* because these words do not identify a specific region or a specific convention.

Has anyone from the Southwestern Region attended the National Sales and Marketing Convention?

> The capital letters indicate a specific region and a specific convention.

Dr. Charles Findleigh was a guest speaker at the National Health Symposium.

> *National Health Symposium* is a specific name. The word *the* and capital letters suggest there is only one symposium.

Dr. Charles Findleigh was a guest speaker at a national health symposium.

> The word *a* before *national* and lower case letters suggest there is more than one symposium.

41

Capitalization

Personal Titles

Capitalize personal titles following a person's name when the title includes the name of a specific department.

> Burt Willson, Vice President of Consumer Products Marketing, presented an overview of this year's objectives.

Remember that capitalizing indicates a special significance within the hierarchy of your organization. Newspapers and magazines do not capitalize most job titles given with department names because these positions are relatively insignificant in the universe of news.

Capitalize titles given with department names when you are referring to anyone else who does business with your organization.

> Shelagh Robinson, Director of Human Resources at Great Company, will call next week to confirm our appointment.

Capitalize personal titles when they are part of the person's name but not when they stand alone or when they are set off by commas.

> Vice President Burt Willson presented an overview of this year's marketing objectives.

>> The title *Vice President* is part of Burt Willson's name just as the title *Mr.* would be.

> The vice president presented an overview of this year's marketing objectives.

> Burt Willson, vice president, presented an overview of this year's marketing objectives.

>> Although lower case is correct in that sentence, use your own judgment to avoid bruising anyone's ego. There may be times, depending on the document and the readers, that you want the special emphasis of capitalized titles.

It is not necessary to capitalize job titles except in announcements or situations meriting special emphasis.

> No one has filled the position of training director.

> Alexander Conroy has accepted the position of Training Director.

You do not need to capitalize job titles even when their acronyms use capital letters.

> All of our customer service representatives (CSRs) will be attending one of the training seminars in July.

Business Style Guide

Capitalization

Locations

Do not capitalize references to floors unless they are in addresses.

> My office is on the ninth floor.
>
> Send the contract to me at the following address:
> 777 Fifth Avenue, 9th Floor, New York, New York 10022.

Capitalize references to geographic parts of the country or the world.

> Until 1990, we did not have any offices in the South.
>
> By September, we will have a Vice President of Information Technology in charge in the Far East.
>
> Our global marketing efforts have had a special emphasis in Eastern Europe.
>
> Is most of your business on the East Coast?

Do not capitalize the words *north, south, east* or *west* when you are indicating a direction.

> To reach the convention center, go east on Route 78 for five miles and take Exit 21.

Seasons

Do not capitalize seasons unless they are part of a specific project.

> When Mackenzie returns in the fall, she will organize a committee to investigate alternatives for working mothers.
>
> July 14 will be this year's Summer Clean Up Day; plan to wear casual clothes so you can help clean out our files.

Publications

Capitalize the first letter of words that are titles of books, magazines, articles, newspapers or movies. Do not capitalize an article (*a, an, the*), conjunction (*and, but, so, or*) or short preposition (*to, in, at, of, for*) unless it begins the title.

> *In Search of Excellence* emphasized that respect for the individual was a pervasive attribute of successful American companies.
>
> Have you read the article on productivity in the most recent *Business Week*?

Capitalization

I've attached "Building a World-Class Organization" from *The Wall Street Journal*.

Refer to page 94 for information about italicizing titles of books and magazines, and to page 136 for information about using quotation marks for titles of articles.

All Capitals

Do not capitalize entire sentences for emphasis. Readability studies have proven that people are distracted by this style. Use boldface or italics instead. If you use all caps in headings, limit them to four or five words.

In e-mail correspondence, using all caps throughout the document is considered shouting and is generally thought to be impolite.

Shortened Forms

Certain organizations or departments use shortened forms of words that are capitalized to indicate specific entities. In the advertising world, it is customary to refer to *the Client* or *the Agency*. These terms are appropriate only in documents where the client's name and the agency's name have already been clearly identified.

In accounting firms, it is common within the organization to refer to *the Firm*. Legal departments and law firms use shortened forms such as *the Company* in contracts to avoid repeating an organization's entire name. These contracts always have an opening paragraph that clarifies the references to these capitalized words.

Business Style Guide

cc

Is it logical to use the notation *cc* when no one uses carbon copies any longer? Yes. Think of the meaning as "courtesy copy," not "carbon copy," and it will make sense.

Some people have suggested using just *c* to indicate *copy*. However, that will not fit with common verbal expressions such as "Please cc me on that." Can you imagine saying, "Please c me on that"?

Alphabetical Order

Most organizations list copy holders in alphabetical order by last name. You may use either an initial and the last name or first and last names. Be sure to use a tab to align all the names.

Top or Bottom

For letters, the cc list is always at the end, after the identification or enclosures line.

> Sincerely,
>
> *Michelle Morrison*
>
> Michelle Morrison
> National Sales Manager
>
> MM:cs
> Enclosures
>
> cc: T. Finholt
>   S. McLean

For memos, the cc list may appear at the bottom of the memo or at the top. Refer to the model memo on page 110.

Blind Carbon Copies

Unless you work in a legal area, you probably will not need to use a blind carbon copy (bcc). A *bcc* indicates that you have sent a copy to someone without telling your primary reader and your cc readers that you have done so.

Colon

Use a colon to introduce lists that are horizontal or vertical.

> I am using three different backup systems: tape, removable cartridge and floppy disk.

> The new approach offers the following benefits:
> - Staff requirements are within our plan.
> - The time required will free up more time for sales.
> - We will have guaranteed customer contact once a week.

> The professional association will:
> - offer quarterly meetings in New York City.
> - lobby Congress for bills that can make a difference in work environment.
> - publish an annual bulletin to send to the membership and the press.

Do not use a colon after the expression *such as* in a sentence.

> Sarah will devote 50% of her time to tasks such as providing project direction and developing reporting procedures.

Use a colon after salutations in business letters even if you use the reader's first name.

> Dear Ms. Ivey:

> Dear Harold:

Use a colon to show that the next statement elaborates on the preceding statement. (A dash is also correct if you want the statement to be emphatic.)

> We have only one objective: success.

Business Style Guide

Comma

Most people use more commas than necessary because they think they need to use one wherever there is a pause. Although readers do tend to pause when they see a comma, you can use specific rules to help you avoid overloading your writing with commas.

Too Many Commas

Commas should help, not hinder, readability. When you use too many commas, you set up stumbling blocks for your reader. Notice how frequently you pause as you read the following paragraph:

> One of the analysts, plans to arrange a meeting, before September 17, to determine a realistic schedule, as we implement the system. Each department representative, serving on the committee, will be expected to present a list of any possible obstacles, to reaching total participation, before the end of the fourth quarter.

Of the eight commas in that paragraph, how many are necessary? None!

Reasons for Commas

There are structural reasons for using commas and for not using commas. If you rely on the rules that are solid, you will be correct most of the time.

If you're not sure that you need one, ask yourself, "What is my reason for putting this comma here?" If your answer is something vague like pausing for a breath, think again. If you can't find a good reason, you may not need a comma at all.

Most of the rules for commas are not open to debate. Since some are, each rule in this chapter has an extra caption in the heading: Always, Never, or Gray Area. The explanation given in each Gray Area will help you decide whether or not you need a comma.

Qualifying Starters — Always

Your readers need to see a comma after certain introductory clauses and phrases to help them understand the relationship of ideas presented in a sentence. When you begin with a qualifying group of words, for example, the comma helps your readers see that you are qualifying.

> Based on what you need, we recommend using the JT Series.
>> The clause starting with *Based* serves to qualify your reason for recommending the JT Series.
>
> As we discussed, the transfer from account #71034 to account #72071 must occur today.
>> The clause starting with *As* tells the reader that he or she knows the information already.

47

Comma

> When you plan your marketing strategy for the exposition, remember that the hours are longer this year.
>
> The clause starting with *When* prepares the reader for the main part of the sentence.

When any of the following words start a sentence, always use a comma after the entire clause or phrase they introduce:

After	*Before*	*Since*
Although	*Despite*	*To*
As	*During*	*When*
Because	*If*	*While*

Place the comma after the entire clause or phrase, not just the introductory word.

> If you have any questions, please call me.
>
> A comma after *If* would not make sense.

Qualifying Endings — Never

The same qualifying groups of words that need commas when they start sentences do not need commas when they end sentences. Therefore, do not use a comma before any of the following words when they occur at the end of a sentence:

after	*before*	*since*
although	*despite*	*to*
as	*during*	*when*
because	*if*	*while*

Since your readers already know the main thought of the sentence before they read the qualifying ending, they don't need a comma to help them understand your message.

> We have hired three new analysts in the department because our workload has increased significantly.
>
>> Use a comma only if you reverse the sentence to start with the word *Because*: **Because our workload has increased significantly, we have hired three new analysts in the department.**
>
> All hiring managers must sign the approval form and send it to Human Resources after the new hire interview.
>
>> You need a comma only if you turn the sentence around: **After the new hire interview, all hiring managers must sign the approval form and send it to Human Resources.**

Business Style Guide

Comma

> Customer responses have been positive despite the initial labeling mistake.
>
> A comma is necessary only if you start with the word *Despite*: Despite the initial labeling mistake, customer responses have been positive.

Contrast or Transition — Always

Certain introductory words or phrases need commas after them because they express contrast or transition from a previous sentence, or they relate to information already known by the reader.

> Unlike many other fat-free products, Nutrifix has no sugar.
>
> Consequently, we chose to move the annual sales meeting to Toronto.
>
> However, the long-term benefits outweigh the short-term expense.
>
> In these situations, it's best to avoid conflict.

Interrupters — Always

You need commas to separate words that add information as a parenthetical thought. The interrupting group of words may rename someone or something, or may add information not essential to the core meaning of the sentence.

> Velma Richards, the associate in charge of this project, will be contacting you within two weeks.
>
>> The interrupting phrase renames Velma; she is now defined by her role as well as by her name.
>>
>> That kind of phrase is called an appositive. It is very common in business correspondence because it's often necessary to give further definition for readers who are not familiar with the subject.
>
> The quarterly financial report, which was expected on Monday, will be available on Wednesday.
>
>> The interrupting clause surrounded by commas gives information that is not essential to the primary meaning of the sentence: The quarterly financial report will be available on Wednesday.

Comma

> Data retrieval, for example, has become relatively easy even for inexperienced users.
>
>> The interrupting phrase surrounded by commas is not essential to the primary meaning of the sentence: Data retrieval has become relatively easy ....
>
> A new voice-mail system, as well as new phones, will be installed on Monday.
>
>> The interrupting phrase surrounded by commas is not essential to the primary meaning of the sentence: A new voice-mail system will be installed ....

Restrictive Expressions — Never

Do not use commas around phrases or clauses that are necessary to limit or define what is being discussed.

> The blue file that is on my credenza is the one you need for database exclusions.
>
>> The clause *that is on my credenza* tells the reader there is only one specific blue file needed for database exclusions. It's possible there are other blue files in the person's office.
>
>> Because the clause limits the subject, it is a restrictive clause. If you used commas to surround it, you would change the meaning of the sentence by suggesting the information is optional.
>
> The consultant selected by our training team will customize the seminar for the Finance Department.
>
>> The phrase *selected by our training team* defines which consultant will customize the seminar. Since the information is essential, commas would not be correct.

Refer to page 161 for an explanation of the differences between *that* clauses not needing commas and *which* clauses requiring commas.

Items in a Series — Gray Area

Everyone knows commas are necessary to separate items in a series. The question that is open to debate has to do with the final comma in the series. Do you always place a comma before the *and*?

When you can leave it out without causing confusion for your reader, leave it out. If you put it in, it's not going to cause any harm.

Business Style Guide

Comma

Wendy needs to create the document, check it for errors, match it with the corresponding invoice and distribute copies to the department.

> Because the reader has heard the verbs *create, check* and *match,* he or she is ready for another verb; it is unlikely that the reader will be confused without a comma after *invoice.*

He asked us to provide descriptions of our services, examples of our assessments, and references.

> The final comma is necessary because the reader could think the writer wants examples of references. Since the goal of good writing is to have the reader get the message instantly, using a comma keeps your reader on track. The reader will not need to go back to examine the sentence.

The Universal Pharmaceutical Company produces Zytec, Abalonz, Permaquid and Miocalc.

> If the reader is familiar with the four different products, there will not be any misunderstanding. If the reader is not familiar with them, you may want a comma after *Permaquid.* This will guarantee that no one thinks there is one product called *Permaquid and Miocalc.*

Our clients include Wonder Company, Global Enterprises, Abbey Construction, and Financial Services of New York.

> Without the comma after *Abbey Construction,* the reader might think there are three clients and that the third client is *Abbey Construction and Financial Services of New York.* If the reader knows the four companies, that misinterpretation is less likely.

The logic behind using commas in a series is that each comma takes the place of the word *and.* Since there is always a final *and,* why should there be a comma along with it?

> The firm's benefits include three weeks' vacation and flex time and summer hours and up to six months for childrearing leave and a subsidized lunch program.
>
> The firm's benefits include three weeks' vacation, flex time, summer hours, up to six months for childrearing leave and a subsidized lunch program.
>
>> Unless you think someone could believe there is up to six months for a subsidized lunch program, a comma between the last two items is unnecessary.

51

Comma

The increasing popularity of vertical lists in business correspondence has eliminated some of the debate on this particular comma rule. If you are concerned that your reader may misinterpret your message, your best choice may be to use a vertical list. Although you may have seen commas in vertical lists, they are unnecessary and, in most cases, distracting. Refer to pages 105 through 106 for more details about punctuation in lists.

Wendy needs to:
- create the document.
- check it for errors.
- match it with the corresponding invoice.
- distribute copies to the department.

He asked us to provide the following:
- descriptions of our services
- examples of our assessments
- references

The Universal Pharmaceutical Company produces the following products:
- Zytec
- Abalonz
- Permaquid
- Miocalc

Our clients include:
- Wonder Company
- Global Enterprises
- Abbey Construction
- Financial Services of New York

The firm's benefits include:
- three weeks' vacation
- flex time
- summer hours
- up to six months for childrearing leave
- a subsidized lunch program

Time or Place Phrases — Gray Area

Some people do not use a comma after a short time or place phrase that starts a sentence. Typical phrases begin with *in* or *at*. If the sentence looks better to you with a comma, go ahead and use it.

At the meeting last week, we discussed alternatives to the current networking arrangement.

Business Style Guide

Comma

Next week, Paula will meet with Steve and Rob to gain a perspective of the new brand.

In New York, there is a coffee shop on every block.

In 1994, we experienced 7% growth in profits.

When you include a specific date, you always need a comma. Refer to pages 62 through 64 for more rules about using dates.

At our meeting on August 31, Constance presented three competitive strategies.

In October 1993, our general manager announced the plans for global reporting.

And, But, and Or *with Two Complete Thoughts — Always*

Use a comma to separate two complete thoughts that are joined by *and*, *but*, or *or*.

The claims adjuster began investigating the claim last week, but he needs to complete his report and recommendation in the next two days.

That sentence has a subject and verb on each side of the word *but*, and each side could stand alone as a complete sentence. In the first part of the sentence, the subject is *adjuster*, and the verb is *began investigating*. In the second part of the sentence, the subject is *he*, and the verb is *needs to complete*.

And, But, and Or *with Two Verbs — Never*

Do not use a comma if the *and*, *but*, or *or* joins two verbs.

The claims adjuster began investigating the claim last week and plans to complete his report and recommendation in the next two days.

That sentence does not have a subject and verb on each side of the word *and*. It simply has two verbs joined by *and*. The subject of the sentence is *adjuster*; the verbs are *began investigating* and *plans to complete*.

Complimentary Closings

Complimentary closings are standard expressions used at the end of letters before your signature and title.

How to Choose the Right Closing

Sincerely is appropriate for all occasions. Don't be concerned about overusing it.

Very truly yours is extremely formal. Top executives use it to distinguish themselves from others.

Best regards is considered good style for international correspondence. If you know the person well, *With warmest regards* is also acceptable.

Respectfully indicates you are subservient to your reader or that you hold your reader in very high esteem. This is a typical closing in writing to government authorities such as judges.

Complimentary closings originated in the days when letters were signed *Your humble servant*. Since times have changed, it's important to choose a closing that fits both the reader and the writer. Most often, that does not include the word *yours*, which indicates possession. Avoid *Sincerely yours*, *Yours truly* and *Respectfully yours*.

Capitalizing, Punctuating and Spacing

Place the complimentary closing on the second line below the last line of the body of your letter. (On your word processor, hit two returns when you finish the last line of your letter.) Capitalize only the first word of the closing, and use a comma at the end of the closing.

The example below illustrates the correct style.

> If you have any questions, please give me a call.
>
> Sincerely,
>
>
> John Canwritewell
> Manager of Technical Service

Complimentary Closings

If your organization uses a style known as open punctuation (Refer to page 120.), you will not use a comma after the complimentary closing. Since this style is not very popular, make sure it has been established as the standard, not just adopted by one or two people.

Letters Only

Do not use complimentary closings in memos. Memos are for internal use only and do not follow the same conventions as letters. Refer to pages 101 and 102 for examples of letter formats, page 110 for a memo format and page 108 for advice on personalizing memos.

International Memos

Although no closing is necessary in a memo, some cultures may find a memo without a closing to be curt. When you're writing a memo to another branch of your company outside the United States, you may add the closing *Best regards* or *Regards*. Avoid more formal closings, however.

Declining Formality?

Everyone knows that in person you would never walk out of your customer's office saying *sincerely*. Nor would you walk in saying *dear*. But, good business requires mutual respect. That's why appointments begin and end with handshakes. It's quite logical that complimentary closings and salutations will last as long as handshakes: forever.

Efforts to encourage a letter format without salutations and complimentary closings have not met with great success. If you use one of these styles, be sure it's acceptable in your organization and your reader's; if not, you risk looking like the uninformed and uneducated one.

complimentary/complementary

If something is *complementary*, it completes or makes up a whole. The connotation is that nothing else is required. In business, the verb form, *complement*, is used more than *complementary*.

> The new division's customized service will complement our major products.

> When we redesigned the office, we realized that the navy blue chairs complement the gray walls in the reception area.

Associate the word *complete* with *complementary* by remembering that both have *e*'s. Ask yourself, "Does this mean complete?" If it does, you need *complementary*.

> Jerry and Ben attribute their success to their complementary management skills.

>> Ben's skills complete Jerry's and vice versa. Together their management skills are complete.

If something is *complimentary*, it praises, expresses gratitude, or is free.

> Complimentary tickets are no longer available.

> To thank you for your order, we have enclosed a complimentary certificate for a dinner at Cher Ami.

> She wrote to the publisher to request a complimentary copy.

> All of us appreciate receiving compliments when we do outstanding work.

Business Style Guide

Contractions

Contractions create an informal conversational style. One or two in a letter can be good, but four or five can be distracting or too casual for business writing. To use contractions appropriately, you need to consider your readers, the nature of the document, and the style you want to convey.

> The brochures I've enclosed give you a detailed review of the services we discussed on the phone.
>> The use of *I've* in a letter to a customer is appropriate; it is also correct, of course, to use *I have*.

The more contractions you use, the more informal you will appear.

Determining the Limits of Informality

Since your writing can still be reader-friendly without contractions, be careful not to use more than you need. Remember that informality has its limits in a business environment. Casual Friday dress codes, for example, have limits in most organizations. Not many have a casual dress code as the norm; one day out of five suggests that casual style is acceptable occasionally. Even on casual days, people often "dress up" for appointments and meetings.

If you're ever in doubt about using contractions, "dress up" your writing. No one will be offended, and your image will not be at risk.

Typical Contractions

The contractions most appropriate for business correspondence are the ones people use every day:

he's	*I'm*	*she's*	*we've*
I'd	*it's*	*they're*	*who's*
I'll	*I've*	*we're*	*you're*

Negatives

The negative form *n't* is one to use sparingly. In most cases where you need to use *n't*, you may need to stress the negative; *not* gives you more emphasis that *n't*.

> The software used in the Purchasing Department does not meet the specifications required in Customer Service.

> If the client chooses both options, do not add the processing charge for both.

> Since we have not received any other complaints about late deliveries, the problem seems to be in your area.

Contractions

Although the ISC link will not be implemented until the end of September, we are making changes now to prepare for a phased approach early next year.

Did the word *not* sound unnatural as you were reading each of those sentences? Probably not. *Doesn't, don't, didn't, can't, haven't, won't* and *weren't* are fine for conversation; use careful judgment in business writing, however.

Technical Writing

If you're in a technical area, your writing does not have to be free of contractions. When you send a memo to a colleague, for example, you may find that contractions are appropriate.

We're reevaluating our Osmosis Monitoring Scheme to include organisms that we have been unable to identify. However, before moving forward, we need to obtain a clear understanding of the tasks involved.

The contraction starting the paragraph makes it sound like a conversation between two people.

Steven Cartwright recently transferred from our Westchester facility to the lab in Cherry Hill. Since he's working on the Pandymonium substrate research, he needs to put in extra time on weekends for the next two months.

The contraction *he's* gives the paragraph a conversational style.

Very few technical descriptions, on the other hand, offer the opportunity for contractions.

Class B initiators run jobs which have a restriction of a maximum of 10 seconds of CPU time. They are more effective than initiators 187 and 188.

Using *They're* instead of *They are* is not necessary and may distract your reader.

Dash

Dashes are popular in advertising copy and in publications known for their superficial treatment of subjects. Since a dash indicates an afterthought or parenthetical information, several dashes in a document can give your reader the impression that you have just thrown thoughts together. To avoid the risk of having your readers perceive you in less than a positive way, use dashes sparingly in business documents.

Note how the following memo relies on dashes as the major form of punctuation:

> As you requested — here's an update on my meeting with Fred Wilkenson.
>
> There are three concerns for next year — turnaround time, overtime costs and billing procedures. He was very firm — but friendly — about getting these items pinned down before he places his January orders.
>
> We need to meet sometime in the next two weeks — if that's convenient for you — to plan our strategy for this account.

Choosing Commas or Colons Instead

If you're using dashes because you are not sure of the correct punctuation, you may want to review the chapters on commas (pages 47 through 53) and colons (page 46). The example on the next page illustrates how you can use commas and colons instead of dashes.

Dash

Do you see a difference in style in the following memo?

> As you requested, here's an update on my meeting with Fred Wilkenson.
>
> There are three concerns for next year: turnaround time, overtime costs and billing procedures. He was very firm, but friendly, about getting these items pinned down before he places his January orders.
>
> We need to meet sometime in the next two weeks, if that's convenient for you, to plan our strategy for this account.

Dramatic Emphasis

Dashes are appropriate for dramatic announcements.

> After six months of trial and error, we finally have the right program — GrammarFix.
>
> > The words *six months* and *finally* suggest there has been some frustration along the way. Using a dash to announce the program is like a trumpet fanfare.

Not Two Hyphens

Word processors allow you to create a solid line as a dash. When typewriters were the norm, everyone used two hyphens. If you're doing this now, others may see you as inexperienced and unaware of current technology; your document will not look as polished as it could.

Em or En Dash

Professional typesetters have always recognized the difference between two kinds of dashes: em and en. Now that word processors give us the same capability, it makes sense to use them appropriately.

Business Style Guide

Dash

An em dash is the one to use for dramatic emphasis. It's about the width of a capital letter *M*.

> In the time management seminar, we received leather desk diaries — not cheap paperback booklets.

An en dash is the one to use when you want to show a range or indicate a duration, but you do not want to use the word *to* or *through*. It's about the width of a capital letter *N*. Since the words *to* and *through* are fine in text, you are more likely to use en dashes in graphs or in listed items.

> The following agenda provides the information you need for the conference:
>
> Monday, September 19
> 8:30 – 9:45   Kick Off Meeting
> 10:00 – 12:00   Training Session with Dr. Wizard
> 12:00 – 1:30   Lunch with the CEO
> 1:30 – 5:30   Presentation of the New Marketing Plan
>
> Tuesday, September 20
> 8:30 – 12:00   Small Group Discussion
> 12:00 – 1:00   Lunch
> 1:00 – 2:30   Concluding Address

Spacing

To surround a dash with spaces or not to use any spaces: that is a cosmetic question you have to answer based on your personal preference.

In the professional publishing arena, you will see both methods used. *The New York Times* uses one space before and after; *The Wall Street Journal* does not use a space on either side. Whatever you decide on, be consistent within a document.

> We plan to introduce four—not two—new products next quarter.
>
> We plan to introduce four — not two — new products next quarter.

61

Dates

Most authorities agree on a majority of the rules for dates. If you notice differences in style within your organization, try to determine if there are any established rules before you use anything that seems too rigid or too casual.

Commas

When the date consists of only the month and the year, do not use a comma between them.

> We expect to complete this work in January 1995.

Always use a comma to separate a month with a number from the year.

> The company became incorporated on August 31, 1987.

You do not need a comma after a date in the middle of a sentence unless there is another logical reason for one.

> The marketing project beginning on December 1, 1994 will extend through February 1995.

> Although the marketing project began in September 1994, it will not be complete until March 1995.

>> You need a comma after *1994* because of the introductory clause starting with *Although.*

When you include the day of the week with a calendar date, you need commas. The calendar date functions as an appositive renaming the day of the week.

> The committee will meet on Wednesday, October 17, to discuss the details of the project.

When the date describes another word, it is not necessary to follow the year with a comma.

> Your April 10, 1994 memo indicated that our audit procedures were being carefully checked.

>> The date describes the word *memo.*

When the month, day and year begin a sentence, use a comma to set off the entire phrase.

> On July 1, 1996, our current CEO will be replaced by our Chief Financial Officer.

Business Style Guide

Dates

Year Too?

As long as the year is obvious from the context of your letter, memo or report, it is not necessary to include it in every date you mention. Keep in mind what you do in everyday conversation. If you tell a colleague on the phone that you are having a meeting on a certain date, do you add the year? Probably not. That's why including the year sometimes changes the tone of a document.

> Thank you for your May 25 letter requesting a credit for finance charges on your April statement.

If your reply is within a week or even a month of the letter you received, your reader will not be confused about the year.

Note how the tone becomes stilted when you include the year.

> Thank you for your May 25, 1994 letter requesting a credit for finance charges on your April statement.

st, nd, rd and th

Do not use *st*, *nd*, *rd* or *th* after a number in a date unless: (1) the number precedes the month, or (2) you refer to the number separately later in a sentence, paragraph or entire document.

> His report was due on the 3rd of February.

> We have two dates available in June: the 22nd or the 29th. July 8 is also open for us.

> Our committee meeting is scheduled for May 11 instead of May 7. If you cannot attend on the 11th, please let me know by the end of this week.

> Give me a call if you have a break in your schedule before the 15th of September.

> Your April 15 report should reflect the recent changes in personnel.

Although most people reading that sentence will say April 15th, you do not need the *th*. The date stands out much more clearly without extra letters.

Abbreviations

Write out the names of days and months. Use abbreviations only for notetaking purposes or for situations where space is an issue. The two or three extra keystrokes are worth it to make your document look as professional as possible.

> Let me know by Monday what your decision is on this issue.

Dates

Slashes

Avoid using slashes with dates: *12/4/94*. This style is too informal for most documents and may result in confusion because of international differences. To Americans, *7/4/95* means *July 4, 1995*. In other countries, however, it means *April 7, 1995*.

If your document requires that you express a period of time known as a season, however, it is acceptable to use slashes.

> During the 1995/96 season, the Metropolitan Opera will present more than 25 different operas with a total of 232 performances.

Military Style or International Style

Unless you are in the military or you work in an international office, there is no reason to put the day before the month and the year: *9 September 1995*. Most American readers will find this distracting and wonder why you don't know the correct style.

Decades

When you need to refer to a time period spanning several years, form the plural by adding *s*, just as you do for most other words.

> In the 1980s, expensive business lunches were common in the financial district. In the '90s, however, expense accounts have been trimmed significantly.
>
> Note that you need an apostrophe before *'90s* to show that you have omitted the *19*.

Centuries

Use a number and a lower case *c* for *century*.

> As we prepare for the 21st century, we recognize that the information superhighway offers technological challenges and legal minefields.

Business Style Guide

different from/different than

Instead of taking time to decide on *from* or *than*, you may want to rewrite the sentence. Frequently, when either expression appears, the sentence is not as substantive as it could be.

> The procedure for recording paid invoices is different from last year's.

> That sentence is correct. However, by rewriting instead of choosing *from* or *than*, you can take the sentence one step beyond the general and get to the specifics that really matter: Our new procedure for recording paid invoices requires much less time than the old one did.

From — *The Safer Choice*

If you learned that *from* is always correct, your teachers found a good way to simplify some complicated grammar. Most of the time, *from* is safe because you will naturally phrase the sentence correctly to fit.

Choose *different from* when you are following the expression with one word or a short phrase that ends with a noun or a pronoun.

> Sari's management style is quite different from Hank's style.

> Our current goals are very different from last year's goals.

Here's why this guideline works: Because *from* is a preposition, it must have a noun or pronoun soon after it to create a prepositional phrase.

> The selections available on CD-ROM are different from the videotape selections.

>> *From the videotape selections* is a prepositional phrase; *from* is the preposition, and the noun is *selections*.

When you use a possessive word, such as *Hank's*, immediately after the word *from*, it is acceptable to end the phrase at that point.

> Sari's management style is quite different from Hank's.

From What

When you use *different from*, you will often follow it immediately with the word *what*.

> The conference was different from what my manager had explained.

65

different from/different than

Than

Although *different than* is correct in certain cases, you are more likely to make a grammatical error when you use it. Unlike the preposition *from*, *than* will not be followed by just one word.

> The alternatives open to working mothers are different than they were fifty years ago.

> That sentence is correct; *than* begins the clause *than they were fifty years ago.*

E-Mail

Although e-mail protocol is still being established, you can avoid the most common problems that have already surfaced.

Stream of Consciousness

Most complaints from senior managers are about the organization of e-mail documents. Because writers tend to write as they think, the message may follow a chronological approach: **Bill called today about .... He said .... I asked .... We decided to ....**

Go ahead and write your message the way you think it. Then, take an extra minute to move your bottom line message to the top: **Bill and I decided to .... When he called today, he said .... I asked ....**

Formatting

The visual impact of an e-mail message may not be as strong as the impact of a hard copy. Until technological improvements are available, rely on three techniques to enhance the format of your message:

- Use headings in all caps to help you create separate sections in a longer message.
- Leave a space between paragraphs to give your reader some breathing room.
- Divide long paragraphs (more than 10 lines of type) into shorter ones (3 to 6 lines) to encourage your reader to keep reading.

E-Mail

Stop Shouting

Have you seen e-mail messages entirely in upper case letters? In the world of e-mail, this is considered shouting. Usually, shouting occurs because the writer hits the Caps Lock key to avoid the extra effort of hitting the Shift key periodically.

Since readability studies have proven it takes longer to read an all upper case message, your extra effort can save others a lot of time.

Are Typos Acceptable?

Contrary to what you may have heard, typos are not acceptable primarily because they interfere with the message. When people notice spelling errors, they tend to think about the mistake, even momentarily, more than the content of the message.

Since early e-mail systems did not make editing as easy as it is now, early users made up their own rule that spelling didn't matter. Every human being makes mistakes when typing quickly. People who do not take an extra minute or two to correct their mistakes, however, generally are perceived as sloppy, lazy or incompetent.

Why put your credibility on the line? You're saving so much time by using e-mail that you can afford to take the time to proofread.

When to Use E-mail Plus a Memo

E-mail works most effectively when the message is short. If readers will have to scan several screens, consider giving an e-mail synopsis and following it with a hard copy full of details.

You can send a brief e-mail message with the bottom line information, but tell your reader a longer memo with complete details is on its way. Using both forms of communicating is especially important because formatting capabilities are, at least for now, much greater in word processing than in e-mail.

Beware of Flaming

The instant nature of e-mail makes it easy to send emotionally charged messages without stopping to think about the consequences. Flaming is the term that has developed to define incendiary messages on e-mail.

If you're angry or annoyed when you are writing an e-mail message, walk away from your computer for a moment. Before you send the message, ask yourself, "Will this message cause more trouble than I want?"

Getting caught in a flame war is usually not productive.

E-Mail

Salutations and Closings

Do not use formal salutations or closings as you do in letters. If you want to personalize the beginning of an e-mail message you are sending to one reader, use the person's name in direct address as you would in person.

If you are making a request and want to end by expressing your appreciation, use the word *Thanks* followed by your name. Use the word *Regards* for messages you send internationally.

> Don,
>
> I need the latest sales figures for all the thermographic products to present to Murray on Friday.
>
> Thanks,
> Carole

Reference Lines

Like a memo, an e-mail message needs a subject or reference line to help your reader quickly identify why you are communicating. Refer to pages 137 through 139 for advice about creating specific reference lines.

Business Style Guide

Ellipsis

Use an ellipsis (...) to let your reader know you have omitted words in a quotation from another document.

> In our annual report, the CEO said he does not expect 1995 to be a "year of ... acquisitions."
>> Because of the ellipsis, readers know that the CEO also offered other words before mentioning acquisitions. The writer chose to leave out those words for a reason, perhaps because the rest of the paragraph or report is going to address acquisitions only.
>
> According to the American Medical Association, private funds provided for research in 1993 had "the greatest impact ... on significant advancement in medical technology."
>> Leave a space before and after an ellipsis unless it ends the sentence.
>
> The e-mail message I received indicated that George was quite disturbed. He said, "No one else has the authority to make that decision ...."
>> The ellipsis tells the reader that George had more to say after the word *decision*. Note that there is no space between the ellipsis and the period at the end of the sentence.

Do not use an ellipsis to indicate a dramatic pause in your writing. Although you may see it used this way in a print advertisement, remember that ad copy is not the same as business correspondence. Advertisers have always taken liberties with words and punctuation to gain a special effect.

To create an ellipsis, use the single character provided on your word processor; do not use three periods. The spacing is slightly closer together with the single character than with three periods.

Ethnic Groups, Races & Nationalities

Capitalize all references to ethnic groups, races and nationalities. Do not use hyphens if a term has two words.

African American *Italian*
American *Latino*
Asian *Mandarin Chinese*
Caucasian *Mexican*
French Canadian *Portuguese*
Hispanic *Spanish*

Leaving out the hyphen carries the connotation that the term is well known to everyone and therefore could not be misunderstood. This is typical of many hyphenated words that do not require hyphens after they become commonplace. *Afro-American*, for example, was a common term in the '70s but, more than two decades later, it is being replaced by *African American*.

> The North American company has recently expanded its manufacturing facilities.

> The French Canadian company moved its headquarters from Quebec to Montreal.

> The company, which is owned by an African American woman, was awarded two major government contracts.

Do not capitalize *black* or *white* if you choose to use those terms, even if you use them as nouns.

Exclamation Point

In business documents you do not have a lot of opportunities to use this dramatic form of punctuation. Used sparingly and appropriately, it adds a touch of enthusiasm to your letters and memos. Overused, it can cause you to appear too casual or even unprofessional.

Decide based on your reader and the subject matter. If you're not sure whether the sentence is dramatic enough for an exclamation point, use a period instead.

Here are some sentences that warrant exclamation points:

> The Midwestern Region more than doubled its sales goal for the second quarter!
>
> Congratulations on your promotion to vice president!
>
> Your presentation today was outstanding!

If you are a very expressive individual and some of your readers are not, be extra sensitive to the possible interpretation on the other end. While your own conversation in person and on the phone may be full of exclamation points, using them on paper is not quite the same. If you are very expressive and everyone you are writing to is also very expressive, exclamation points are more likely to be well received.

farther/further

In most business situations, you need to use *further*, not *farther*.

Additional *or* More

When you mean "additional" or "more," use *further*.

> If you need further information, please give me a call.
>
> Process the order without any further delay.

Remembering the word *furthermore* may help you to remember that *further* means "more."

> Furthermore, we cannot accept lower quality standards and expect to continue building market share.
>
> The meaning of *furthermore* is "in addition."

Another choice is to use the word *more* instead of *further*. That's a word you will never misuse.

> If you need more information, please give me a call.

To a Greater Extent

To express distance in a figurative sense meaning "to a greater extent," use *further*.

> With the exchange rate, the dollar goes further in Canada.
>
> The dollar is not actually traveling down the road!

Actual Distance

Choose *farther* when you are referring to miles or kilometers or some other unit of measure for actual distance.

> The office complex is two miles farther down the road.
>
> She traveled 150 miles farther than she had planned on the first day of her field supervision.

fewer/less

Be careful of using *less* when you need *fewer*. *Less* is correct when you are talking about something that is a mass, not separate items. Associate the *ss* in *less* with the *ss* in *mass*.

We have less inventory at this point than we did last year.

Use *fewer* when you can count items individually. Associate the *er* in *fewer* with the *er* in *number*.

Fewer accidents last year reduced our insurance premiums.

How many accidents occurred last year? You could provide the exact number.

Decide based on the actual word that *less* or *fewer* describes. Sometimes the same subject can be expressed in two ways; one may need *fewer*, and the other may need *less*.

Our new office location has allowed me to put fewer miles on my car.

How many miles have you driven the car? You can respond with a specific number.

Our new office location has allowed me to put less mileage on my car.

Although you can count miles, mileage is considered a mass.

Use *less* when you refer to periods of time or amounts of money.

Computerizing the operation will require less than six months.

Although you can count how many months a project will take, the period of time is considered a mass, not separate items.

With less than $500 in the account, this client is jeopardizing his preferred status.

Although you can count the bills making up the sum of $500, the entire amount is considered a mass.

Fonts

Typewriters allowed almost no flexibility in typeface size or style. Now that personal computers offer so many options under the Font menu, you may not be sure what to choose.

If your organization has established a style for all correspondence, follow those guidelines. If not, use the advice in this chapter to help you make your own decisions. Above all, remember that the document that looks good is the document that gets read before others.

Understanding Fonts

To choose the right font, you need to understand three terms: serif, sans serif and proportional.

Serif fonts incorporate small strokes, called serifs, at the ends of each letterform to guide the reader's eye from character to character. This allows readers to comprehend words and sentences instead of individual letters.

Sans serif fonts do not have the small strokes as part of the letterform design; the word *sans* means "without." The headings in this book are set in a proportional sans serif font, part of the Futura family.

Proportional fonts allot different widths to letters. *I*, for example, takes up less space than *M*. This paragraph is set in Garamond, a proportional serif font.

Using Fonts Effectively

For most business documents, use only one serif font for both text and headings. Readability studies have proven that, for more than a few words of text, serif fonts such as Times or Garamond are easier to read than sans serif fonts such as Helvetica.

Since sans serif fonts are more readable in small doses, they are effective in headings. A sans serif heading also provides visual contrast to text set in a serif font. If you are creating a special document such as a manual or proposal, or if you can take the time to add visual variety to your document, use a sans serif font for headings.

Spacing Between Sentences

Because the type on typewriters was not proportional, two spaces were necessary between sentences for ease of reading. Proportional fonts, however, require only a single space; two spaces create gaps that interfere with readability. Use only one space, not two, between sentences.

Business Style Guide

Fonts

Type Size

Use 10 or 12 point type for correspondence. Larger sizes look amateurish. When computer printers did not produce fine quality type, people sometimes used larger point sizes to make documents more readable. Laser printers and ink jet printers, however, produce such sharp resolution that 10 or 12 point is very clear.

What to Avoid

Although it is a serif font, avoid Courier because it is monospaced, with every letter and space of equal width. Documents created in Courier look just like typewritten documents; they are relics!

```
This example of Courier type illustrates
how each letter takes up the same amount
of space.
```

Do not combine two serif or two sans serif fonts in the same document. In most cases, the designs of the two fonts will "compete" with each other, making your document less readable.

Unless you have had some training in graphic design, do not mix several font styles and sizes in one document.

> Experimenting with font styles can be dangerous. Have you seen documents that look like *ransom* notes?

Related References

To add to your understanding of visual impact, refer to the following chapters:

Capitalization	page	39
Headings	page	84
Italics	page	94
Letters	page	97
Lists	page	104
Memos	page	108
Paragraphs	page	120

75

formally/formerly

When you remove the *ly* from either of these words, you probably do not have doubts about which word you want. That's the easiest way to decide the word that fits. Are you talking about something that is *formal* or something that was *former*?

> My former boss encouraged me to check with her frequently while I worked on projects. My current boss prefers that I save most information for my monthly report.

> Derek Knudson, formerly of Zwick Associates, is joining our firm next month.

>> Derek used to be with Zwick, but he is not there any longer.

> Since the gala event required formal attire, I needed to rent a tuxedo.

> As a result of our conversation today, I have formally withdrawn our offer to complete the work for $300,000.

>> That could be the opening line of a letter or memo documenting the decision.

Business Style Guide

Fragments

To meet the requirements of a complete sentence, a group of words must: (1) have a subject and verb, and (2) express a complete thought. When a group of words does not meet these two requirements, it's called a fragment.

> In reference to your letter about the system upgrade.
>> That fragment leaves the reader hanging.
>
> I received your letter about the system upgrade.
>> That sentence expresses a complete thought. *I* is the subject and *received* is the verb.

Most fragments in business correspondence occur because people change their minds while they are typing, and they forget to proofread carefully.

> Harold working harder than any other person in the group.
>> Did you automatically think the writer made a typing or proofreading error? A missing verb causes most readers to react with the thought, "This doesn't make sense." The reader must then take a moment to pick an appropriate verb: Harold is working .... or Harold was working .... or Harold has been working .... or Harold will be working ....

Although you may see fragments starting with *which* in some books and periodicals, avoid this style in business. In most cases you can use the word *this* instead and end up with a complete sentence.

> Which had a positive effect on the first phase of the project.
>> That fragment needs to be either part of the sentence it follows or a separate sentence: This had a positive effect on the first phase of the project.

graduated/was graduated

Use just the word *graduated* and you will never be wrong. Note that you need the word *from* when you give the name of the institution.

> The marketing analyst graduated from Dartmouth last year.
>
> Scott graduated summa cum laude from the University of Pennsylvania.

Some sources also endorse the expression *was graduated* as long as the word *from* is included. However, *was graduated* is passive voice. It sounds strange to most ears and gives the credit to the institution as opposed to the person who graduated.

have/has/had

In their role as helping verbs, *have*, *has* and *had* often affect the precise meaning of a sentence. Understanding them can help you choose the verb form you need.

Has and Have

When you use *has* or *have* with a verb in the past tense, you are using the present perfect tense.

> Mona has investigated the claim.

> The candidates have prepared short presentations for the review committee.

The present perfect tense suggests that a past action has just occurred, or continues up to the present time.

> Lyle has accepted a position with one of our subsidiaries.
>> The use of *has* suggests that Lyle just accepted the position. Lyle accepted a position ... is also correct, but the past tense does not imply that the action occurred recently.

> I have commuted to work for five years.
>> The use of *have* suggests that I still do commute. I commuted to work ... is also correct, but the past tense implies that I no longer commute.

This tense also indicates that the action occurred at an indefinite time in the past.

> I have lived in several cities.
>> Perhaps I still live in a city. Perhaps I am referring to a time period of months or years.

> I have called the technical support department several times, but no one has resolved the problem.
>> Perhaps I just called a moment ago. Perhaps I called last week or yesterday or earlier today.

I Have Enclosed

Since the expression *I have enclosed* is a very common opening line in business, it may help you to recognize why the word *have* is necessary. The nature of a letter or memo is such that the reader of the document hears the writer speaking. An opening line in the past tense would suggest that the letter is finished before it actually gets going.

Business Style Guide

have/has/had

I enclosed the report ....

> That opening suggests the action was completed in the past. It does not sound as though the writer is going to continue speaking. The writer sounds as though he or she has finished the letter.

I have enclosed the report ....

> That opening suggests that the writer is going to continue talking. The action just happened. It is impossible to add *yesterday* or *last week*.

When *I have enclosed* appears in the middle or at the end of a memo or letter, it's appropriate because the writer has not finished speaking.

How Tense Affects Meaning

Present perfect tense differs only slightly in meaning from past tense. However, your reader will detect this difference. Note the contrast in two examples from an audit report.

> Accounts Receivable has developed a procedure to flag accounts that are delinquent by more than 30 days. The anticipated effect is to reduce the need for manual checking and decrease the turnaround time for sending second invoices.
>
>> Because *has developed* suggests the action occurred recently, the reader expects an answer to the question, "What is that going to do?"
>
> Accounts Receivable developed a procedure to flag accounts that are delinquent by more than 30 days. It reduced the need for manual checking and decreased the turnaround time for sending second invoices.
>
>> Because *developed* suggests the action did not occur recently, the reader expects an answer to the question, "What did that do?"

have/has/had

Switching Tenses

You often need to use the present perfect tense in the first sentence of memos and letters. The second sentence, however, may switch to another tense.

Note in the following example that you can begin with the present perfect tense and then move to present tense:

> I have reviewed the material you sent me. Although your new information services package seems to be very thorough, I do not see a need for it in our department.

Note in the following example that you can begin with the present perfect tense and then move to future tense:

> I have enclosed the material you requested. Since we will be updating several of these brochures in the next month, I will make sure you receive the new versions as soon as they are available.

Two Common Mistakes

The most common mistake people make with the present perfect tense is to include a definite time in the same sentence.

> I have reviewed the material you sent me.

>> It would not be correct to assign a definite time in that sentence: Yesterday I have reviewed the material you sent me. The use of *have* suggests that the reviewing could have occurred at any time.

> Elaine reviewed all of our standard operating procedures for clarity when she was in charge of the department.

>> Since there is a definite time in the past when Elaine did the reviewing, past tense is the only verb form that fits. It would not be correct to say: Elaine has reviewed all of our standard operating procedures ... when she was in charge of the department.

The other mistake people make is to use the simple past tense when they need the present perfect tense to suggest an action is continuing.

> For the past year, our research focused on a formula to reduce the amount of fat in WonderButter.

>> That sentence is grammatically correct. If the research is continuing, however, the sentence does not convey the correct meaning. The verb *focused* in the past tense suggests that the research is over.

Business Style Guide

have/has/had

> For the past year, our research has focused on a formula to reduce the amount of fat in WonderButter.
>> That sentence is also grammatically correct. Using *has focused* in the present perfect tense, however, tells your reader that the research is continuing.

Errors in Speaking

Since errors with *has* and *have* sometimes occur in speaking, check the following list to make sure you know what is correct:

Not Correct	Correct
I seen it	*I have seen it*
he done it	*he has done it*
she has went	*she has gone*
we would have went	*we would have gone*
she should have spoke	*she should have spoken*
he has did the work	*he has done the work*

Had

The most common mistake people make with *had* is to use it when they don't need it. The past perfect tense (*had* with a verb in the past tense) is correct only when you need to emphasize that one past action occurred before another past action.

> If Rick had known about the company's relocation plans, he might not have accepted the position.
>> The use of *had* along with *known* clarifies that Rick would have learned about the relocation plans before he accepted the position.

> I had analyzed the data to find the bug in the system.
>> That sentence is not correct. Since no other past action occurred, the sentence should be: **I analyzed the data** ….

> My administrative assistant had worked in that department for five years.
>> That sentence is not correct. Since no other past action occurred, the sentence should be: **My administrative assistant worked in that department** ….

... have/... of

If you see someone use *of* instead of *have*, the cause could be poor proofreading. The sound of the word *of* is so similar to the sound of *have* used as a contraction that the mistake is more common than people would like to admit.

> Stefan could have completed the project in two days.
>> In conversation, you might say: **Stefan could've** (pronounced like *could of*) **completed the project** ....

he/she/him/her

The mistakes that occur with these pronouns cause listeners and readers to react as though they have just heard fingernails against a chalkboard. Unfortunately, the people who make the mistakes are generally unaware that anything is wrong.

Take Out the Word I

If you do not realize that the following sentence is incorrect, try reading it without the reference to yourself.

> Her and I will schedule a meeting for next month.
>> That sentence is not correct. Would you say: **Her will schedule a meeting for next month?**

> She and I will schedule a meeting for next month.
>> That sentence is correct. If you had thought about using *Her* and you took out *and I*, you would realize that *Her will schedule ...* does not sound right. *She* functions as part of the subject of the sentence.

> When he and I met with the training group, we presented a list of the top ten priorities.
>> That sentence is correct. If you had thought about using *him* and you took out *and I*, you would realize that *When him met ...* does not sound right. *He* functions as part of the subject in the clause starting with *When*.

he/she/him/her

Subjects vs. Objects

You need *he* and *she* as subjects (doers). You need *him* and *her* as objects (words that receive action). Most of the situations that require *him* and *her* are simple ones that never cause any problems.

> Please contact her if you have any questions.
>> You don't need to know that *her* is the direct object of *contact*. Your ear tells you that *her* is correct.
>
> When you meet with him next Friday, ask about his plans to expand that segment of the business.
>> You don't need to know that *him* is the object of the preposition *with*. Your ear tells you that *him* is correct.

Caution with Before, After and Than

If you know that the people you communicate with are very particular about correct grammar, do not trust your ear when you use the words *before*, *after* and *than*. A common mistake is to use *him* or *her* when *he* or *she* is correct.

It is not correct to say *than him* or *than her*.

> I usually work later than her.
>> That sentence is not correct. It should be: I usually work later than she does.

If *than her* and *than him* sound correct to you, you are possibly being influenced by television characters. The people who entertain you as you recline in your easy chair may not be good role models for business communication.

Unless you mean "in front of," *before him* or *before her* is not correct.

> I often leave the office before him.
>> That sentence is not correct. It should be: I often leave the office before he does.
>
> Jackie said she was ready to meet the challenges before her.
>> The challenges are in front of Jackie.
>
> I offered the suggestion before she did.
>> That sentence is correct. However, it would not be correct to say: I offered the suggestion before her.

he/she/him/her

Unless you mean "behind," *after him* or *after her* is incorrect.

> I often leave the office after him.
>> That sentence is not correct. It should be: I often leave the office after he does.
>
> I received the memo after he did.
>> That sentence is correct. However, it would not be correct to say: I received the memo after him.

Most of the situations you have in business will not require a reference to being "in front of" or "behind." They are much more likely to concern actions that occur before or after other actions.

Avoiding Sexist Writing

Pages 168 and 169 explain how to include both male and female references without overusing *he/she* and *him/her*.

Headings

Because most business readers want to skim documents, headings can make that easy for them. Headings can also help you organize your thoughts.

Minimum Requirement: Two

Make sure you have at least two headings in a document; just one does not make sense.

No Underlines

Use boldface or italics but not underlining. Underlining obscures the descenders, those parts of the letters *g, j, p, q* and *y* that fall below the printed line.

When everyone used typewriters, the primary way to distinguish headings was to use underlining. Word processors, however, make it simple to create more professional-looking documents. The more your readers see better quality documents, the higher their expectations are for all documents.

Headings

Letters and Numbers

Avoid using Roman numerals or letters next to headings. Unless people must refer to particular sections by number and letter, you can usually do without them. The words by themselves will stand out for your reader.

Specific, Not General

Your readers can gain more information from a heading that says:

> Why XYZ Corporation is the Best Choice

than they can from:

> Choices Considered

or:

> Methodology

Typefaces

Do not use a type size that is significantly larger than your text. Usually the same size gives you the most professional look.

Although it is not necessary for most business documents, you can create a stronger impression by using two different fonts: one for headings and one for text. Most professional typesetters use a sans serif font for headings and a serif font for the text.

Refer to page 75 for more explanation about fonts.

All Caps

Since readability studies have proven it's easier for people to read a combination of upper and lower case than all upper case, limit your use of all caps to headings of three or four words.

hopefully

This word has been misused so much that you will rarely hear it used correctly. Your best choice is to replace it with something stronger and more appropriate for business.

> The immigrants looked hopefully at the Statue of Liberty as they entered New York's harbor.

The word *hopefully* is correct in that sentence. It means "full of hope" or "in a hopeful manner." How often do you have an opportunity in business documents to talk about people looking *hopefully* at something?

> Hopefully, we will settle the labor dispute tomorrow.

That sentence is typical of what you hear people say. However, it sounds very weak when you hear it with the definition of *hopefully*: Full of hope, we will settle the labor dispute tomorrow.

Here are two better choices for business: **We expect to settle the labor dispute tomorrow**, or **We plan to settle the labor dispute tomorrow**. Expectations and plans are appropriate for business; hopes do not convey the same strength.

however

However is a good word to help you illustrate a contrast in thought. You can use it four ways:

- To start a sentence.

    The bookshelves for your office were ordered three months ago. However, the company has experienced production problems that will delay delivery another two weeks.

- To start an independent clause after a semicolon.

    Several candidates have applied for the position; however, only two have the qualifications we want.

- To interrupt in the middle of other words.

    Electric typewriters saved time compared to manual typewriters in the 1960s. Word processors, however, have significantly surpassed the capabilities of electric typewriters.

- To end a sentence.

    Michael has the technical expertise required for the position. He does not have the social skills, however.

If you receive the feedback that you are overusing *however*, consider *although* as an alternative to start the sentence.

Although the bookshelves for your office were ordered three months ago, the company has experienced production problems that will delay delivery another two weeks.

Although several candidates have applied for the position, only two have the qualifications we want.

Although electric typewriters saved time compared to manual typewriters in the 1960s, word processors have significantly surpassed the capabilities of electric typewriters.

Although Michael has the technical expertise required for the position, he does not have the social skills.

Hyphenated Words

The hyphen lets you create one word out of two or three. Since some words lose their hyphens as they become familiar to a wide audience, the rules for hyphenating can be confusing.

Your primary concern needs to be readability. If you do not see a rule in this chapter that fits your situation and you think a term is more easily recognizable with a hyphen, use one.

Form Follows Function

Your decision to hyphenate usually depends on the function that the word has in the sentence. When a hyphenated word modifies or describes the word immediately following it, the hyphenated word functions as a compound adjective.

> Two one-day conferences will address the major questions about ethics in the workplace.
>
> The word *one-day* describes *conferences.*
>
> A four-person committee will review and refine evaluation methods.
>
> The word *four-person* describes *committee.*
>
> The Chicago-based organization has increased its profits by 21% in the last year.
>
> The word *Chicago-based* describes *organization.*

The purpose of the hyphen is not to announce to the world that you know this new word is a compound adjective, of course. Its purpose is clarity. In most cases, the hyphen helps your reader link the two words as one.

> Ariel has developed a new training program that provides hands-on experience with the integrated system.
>
>> The hyphen in *hands-on* makes it easy for readers to link that word with the word *experience.* If there were no hyphen, someone could possibly link the word *provides* with the word *hands*: ... a training program that provides hands ....

Since people read clusters of words at a time, especially when they are skimming documents, hyphenating a word can keep your reader moving quickly through the document. If your reader must pause, even for a moment, to determine the relationship of words, he or she is not focusing on your overall message.

Business Style Guide

Hyphenated Words

Often, two words that are not hyphenated look exactly like those that are hyphenated. The difference is probably that the nonhyphenated words function as a noun or as a verb and the hyphenated words function as an adjective.

> Rami has added valuable insight to the decision-making process.
>> The word *decision-making* is an adjective modifying *process*.
>
> Janice's performance appraisals for the last three years indicate that she has a problem with decision making.
>> The words *decision making* function as a compound noun, not a compound adjective, and no hyphen is necessary.
>
> Our follow-up procedures will ensure that everyone complies with the new policy.
>> The word *follow-up* is an adjective modifying *procedures*.
>
> We need to follow up on a regular basis.
>> Since the words *follow up* function as a verb, no hyphen is necessary.

Compound Adjectives After a Noun

Most of the time you will use a compound adjective before the noun you are describing.

> We need to gather up-to-date information.
>> The compound adjective *up-to-date* modifies the word *information*. Using the hyphens helps your reader cluster all three words as a unit rather than link the word *gather* with the word *up*: We need to gather up ....

If you place a compound adjective after the noun it modifies, do not use hyphens unless the adjective ends in *ed*, *en* or *ing*.

> The information we have gathered is up to date.
>> The words *up to date* still describe *information*, but because they occur after *information*, there is no need for hyphens.
>
> The Customer Service Department has spent two months revising its model letters to ensure that all correspondence is customer-focused.
>> The word *customer-focused* describes *correspondence*. Because the word *focused* ends in *ed*, you need to hyphenate the compound word.

89

Hyphenated Words

Mid

Use a hyphen with the prefix *mid* when you refer to a specific time.

mid-eighties   *mid-1995*

Do not hyphenate other words using *mid* as a prefix.

midcareer   *midstream*
midsized   *midyear*

Re

Hyphenate words starting with the prefix *re* only when there could be confusion for the reader.

> Our Communications Department has reformatted the company stationery.

Readers will not be confused by *reformatted*.

> The manufacturer needed to re-form the mold used to create the trial size bottles.

Since *reform* is a common word, using the hyphen draws the reader's attention to the word *re-form*.

> Re-engineering efforts this year have resulted in layoffs of 2500 people in five plants.

If your organization has gone through a reengineering process, probably no one uses the hyphen any longer. As long as your readers have seen the word frequently, they will not be thrown by the two *e*'s together.

Most other words using *re* do not need hyphens.

recalculate   *reorder*
remodel   *reorganize*

Non

Since words using the prefix *non* are so common, it is not necessary to use hyphens.

> Nonprofit organizations do not use the same procedures for financial reporting.

The term *not-for-profit* is always hyphenated, however, because three words written as one would look strange.

Hyphenated Words

Multi

This prefix is another example of one that is so familiar there is no need to use hyphens.

multicultural   *multipurpose*
multifaceted   *multinational*

Numbers

Hyphenate two-word numbers expressed as words but not three-word numbers.

twenty-seven   *three hundred fifty*

Financial Terms

A number of terms in the financial world are hyphenated. Although some of them may seem clear to you without hyphens, keep in mind that precision is extremely important in this area. Rather than risk misunderstanding, most financial professionals use hyphens. Here are several of the most common expressions:

asset-backed   *short-term*
below-market   *year-end*
price-to-earnings   *before-tax*

Words with ly

When you describe something by using a word ending in *ly* along with another word, do not hyphenate the two words. Most words ending in *ly* are adverbs modifying adjectives.

clearly defined

Together these two words may describe a word such as *objectives*, but *clearly* is an adverb modifying *defined*.

extremely positive

Together these two words may describe a word such as *feedback*, but *extremely* is an adverb modifying *positive*.

poorly conceived

Together these two words may describe a word such as *plan*, but *poorly* is an adverb modifying the word *conceived*.

widely accepted

Together these two words may describe a word such as *practice*, but *widely* is an adverb modifying the word *accepted*.

Hyphenated Words

Miscellaneous Terms

Do not hyphenate words referring to a particular group of people. (Refer to page 70 about references to ethnic groups and nationalities.)

> The African American owner received an award from the National Association of Women Business Owners.

Do not hyphenate words identifying a century.

> Undoubtedly, 21st century advertisers will have clearly defined road signs and rules for the information superhighway.

Word Division

If your writing requires a lot of hyphenated words, you may want to be extra conscious of words that you divide because they do not fit on one line. Avoid ending more than two consecutive lines of type with a hyphen. With word processors, it's easy to keep a whole word on one line, to force a word onto the next line or to eliminate automatic word division entirely.

Business Style Guide

i.e. and e.g.

Your writing will be clearer without these Latin abbreviations. If you use them because they are accepted in your particular field, limit their use to items given in parentheses, and make sure you use them correctly. The meaning of *i.e.* is "that is" from the Latin *id est*; *e.g.* means "for example" from the Latin *exempli gratia*.

Note that neither of them means "such as." It's typical to translate them that way, however, when you use words instead of the abbreviations.

> The change in structure will help our organizations work together in several key ways (e.g., integrating training resources, providing new job opportunities and developing compatible systems).

> The change in structure will help our organizations work together in several key ways. For example, we can integrate training resources, provide new job opportunities and develop compatible systems.

> The change in structure will help our organizations work together in several key ways, such as integrating training resources, providing new job opportunities and developing compatible systems.

The correct form for *i.e.* and *e.g.* requires periods, no space between the letters, and a comma before the words that follow.

> i.e.,

> e.g.,

imply/infer

You can imply something only when you are the writer or the speaker. You can infer something only when you are the reader or the listener.

Imply means "suggest"; *infer* means "draw a conclusion."

> My manager implied that there would be additional layoffs later in the year.
>> The manager is doing the suggesting.

> My manager inferred from the report that there would be additional layoffs later in the year.
>> The manager came to a conclusion based on information provided by someone else.

Italics

Word processors have given us the capability to use the same distinctions professional typesetters have always used. If you learned to use underlining instead of italics, remember that the equipment you were using could not produce italics. Because underlining obscures the descenders of the letters *g, j, p, q* and *y*, it hinders readability.

Titles

Italicize titles of books, magazines, newspapers, movies and pamphlets.

> *Fortune* is known for its accurate ratings of companies.
>
> I have *The New York Times* delivered to my office.
>
> *The Elements of Style* is a popular reference book.
>
> Our communications director published a pamphlet called *The Success of Managed Care in the Nineties* to distribute to all our clients.
>
> *Gone With the Wind* is a classic film.

Words Singled Out

Italicize words, numbers or letters of the alphabet being singled out.

> *Recommendation* has only one *c* but two *m*'s.

Extra Emphasis

Use either italics or boldface to distinguish items as extra important in text. Either style is better than using all upper case or underlining.

> The new system software will be available for everyone on March 1. Please use the next two weeks to do some housekeeping on the network. Discard all files that you no longer need to have. *Remember the more space you clear, the more will be available for you!*

Mechanical Details

If your goal is the most professional appearance possible, you may want to know about the finer details of italicizing.

- Italicize the space before the word you are italicizing. Although the difference is subtle, the spacing will be in better proportion.
- Do not italicize the space after the word you are italicizing.
- Italicize the punctuation after an italicized word only if the word is part of a completely italicized sentence. Depending on the font you are using, you may have to kern (subtly adjust the spacing of) the punctuation after the italicized word.

its/it's

The word *its* is called a possessive pronoun; it indicates ownership.

> The group has established its objectives.
>> The objectives belong to the group.
>
> The magazine has changed its appearance dramatically since the early '70s.
>> The appearance belongs to the magazine.

The word *it's* is a contraction for *it is*. The apostrophe indicates that a letter is missing.

> It's unfortunate that you could not attend the meeting.
>> That sentence says: It is unfortunate ....
>
> When I called Jaime to thank him for his participation in the project, he said, "It's always a pleasure to work with you."
>> That sentence says: It is always a pleasure ....

Why People Get Confused

If you have trouble distinguishing these two words, stop to consider why you do. Most of the time you use nouns when you indicate possession. Nouns always require apostrophes to form the possessive.

> Hannah's performance appraisal was extremely positive.
>> *Hannah* is a noun. To form the possessive, you add an apostrophe and *s*.
>
> The company's policy is to include psychological testing as part of the screening process.
>> *Company* is a noun. To form the possessive, you add an apostrophe and *s*.

Pronouns do not follow the same rules as nouns to show possession.

> His performance appraisal was extremely positive.
>> *His* is the possessive form of the pronoun *he*.
>
> Its policy is to include psychological testing as part of the screening process.
>> *Its* is the possessive form of the pronoun *it*.

its/it's

Mental Trick to Remember

It may help you to remember that *its* is like *his*. They both show possession (*his plans* or *its plans*, for example). Try substituting *his* to see if it would fit grammatically if you were talking about a person instead of a thing.

> The group has established its objectives for next year.
>
>> If you substitute *his* for *its*, the sentence could make sense grammatically: He has established his objectives for next year.
>
>> This mental substitution tells you that *its* is correct.

lend/loan

Depending on your audience, you may receive a strong negative reaction if you misuse these words. Play it safe and recognize that they are used in slightly different ways.

Lend

Choose *lend* or the past tense *lent* as a verb when someone borrows anything including money.

> Banks have become reluctant to lend money to entrepreneurs without sufficient collateral.
>
> Alexis lent me the software on a trial basis.

Loan

Loan is always correct as a noun.

> His new company received a loan of $25,000 from the Small Business Association.

If you work in a financial institution where *loan* has become acceptable as a verb, remember to restrict its use to financial settings only.

> The bank was willing to loan up to $50,000 for minority-owned businesses.
>
> Mr. Maguire's bank loaned him $10,000 to use as a draw against his company's receivables.

Business Style Guide

Letters

When you do not follow the accepted format for a letter, you risk having your readers perceive you and your organization as unprofessional. Like your organization's annual report and other promotional literature, your letter may be circulated to others and may stay in the file long after the subject it addressed is closed.

Letters:

- are for all correspondence outside your organization.
- belong on official letterhead.
- have an inside address.

    Person
    Title
    Company
    Address

- begin with a salutation.

    Dear Ms. ...:

- end with a complimentary closing.

    Sincerely,

    Your Name
    Your Title

Standard Styles

The decision to use block style (all parts of the letter aligned to the left) or modified block style (date, closing and signature centered) depends on the layout of your stationery and an accepted style established within your organization. Examples of each style appear on pages 101 and 102.

Block style is preferred when the letterhead is aligned to the right; when the letterhead is left-aligned or centered, either style is acceptable.

Block style is more popular because it's slightly easier for people who produce their own documents on personal computers. Aligning everything to the left lessens the need to set tabs and usually results in fewer keystrokes.

Letters

Typing vs. Word Processing

Long-established format rules for typewriters still apply to word processing. The major difference regarding format has to do with terms and techniques. To offer practical advice for the majority of people who continue to use a typewriter operating style, this chapter gives directions for vertical spacing by referring to inches and numbers of lines. If you are accustomed to word processing terminology, you can adapt the directions accordingly.

Date Line

If your date line is too close to the letterhead or too close to the inside address, your letter looks crowded and you look like an amateur.

Give your reader about a half inch of white space between your letterhead information and the date.

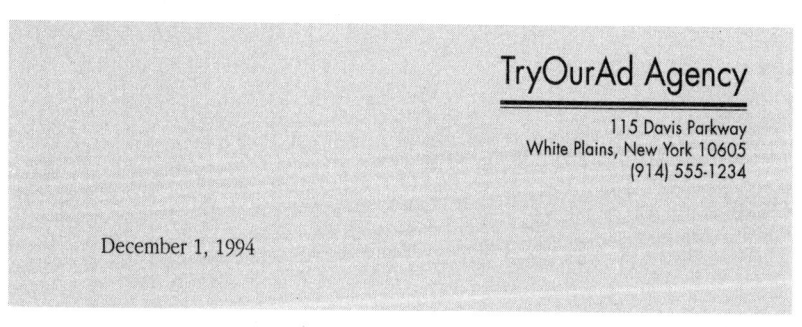

> **TryOurAd Agency**
> 115 Davis Parkway
> White Plains, New York 10605
> (914) 555-1234
>
> December 1, 1994

Inside Address

Leave at least three lines between the date and the inside address. If your letter is short, you can leave as many as six lines to avoid a top-heavy letter.

> December 1, 1994
>
> Mr. Darren Hughes
> Vice President
> Executive Resources
> 212 Grand Avenue
> Pinehurst, North Carolina 28374

The space between the date and the inside address is your primary place for adjustments to fit more or less on one page.

Business Style Guide

Letters

Vertical Spacing

Single space all letters, even short ones. Double space between paragraphs and between:

- the inside address and the salutation.
- the salutation and the first line of the letter.
- the last line of the letter and the complimentary closing.
- the writer's title and the typist's initials or enclosure notation.
- the typist's initials or enclosure line and the cc list.

If you use a reference line, double space before and after it. For more information about reference lines, refer to pages 137 through 139.

> Mr. Darren Hughes
> Vice President
> Executive Resources
> 212 Grand Avenue
> Pinehurst, North Carolina 28374
>
> Re: August 1995 Sales Meeting
>
> Dear Mr. Hughes:

After the complimentary closing, leave three lines for your signature. Note the example on the next page.

Margins

Use one-inch left and right margins, and leave at least one inch at the bottom of the page.

Do not right justify margins. In most cases, justified right margins cause undesirable vertical "rivers" of white space. Word processors struggle unsuccessfully to space words appropriately to create the justified margin. In books, justified margins are common, but copy editors take the time to subtly adjust lines to avoid awkward spacing. In newspapers, justified margins are necessary because the type is set in columns.

More than One Page

For page 2 of a letter, do not use letterhead. Make a header by typing the addressee's full name at the left, centering the word *Page* followed by a space and the page number, and right justifying the date.

Letters

Leave two blank lines after this header, and always make sure you have at least two lines of text before the closing.

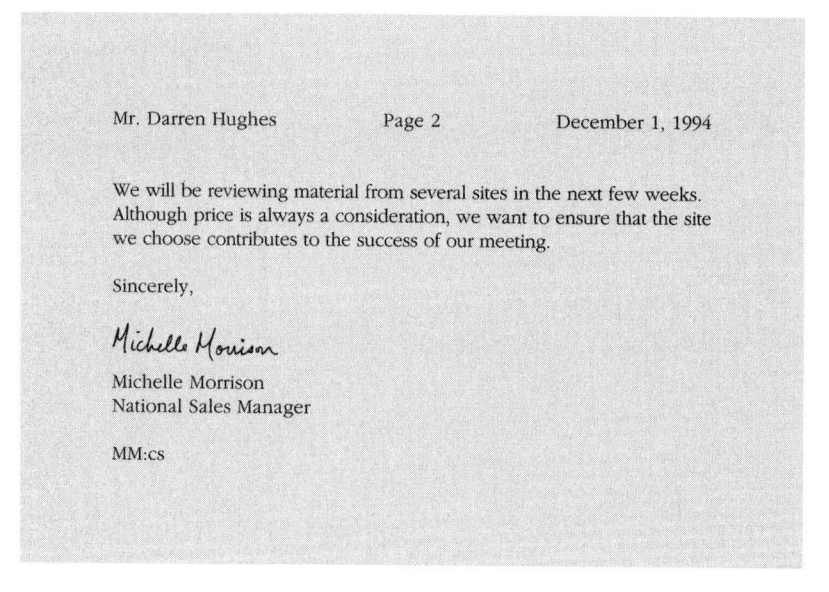

> Mr. Darren Hughes   Page 2   December 1, 1994
>
> We will be reviewing material from several sites in the next few weeks. Although price is always a consideration, we want to ensure that the site we choose contributes to the success of our meeting.
>
> Sincerely,
>
> *Michelle Morrison*
>
> Michelle Morrison
> National Sales Manager
>
> MM:cs

If your organization uses a preprinted second sheet, you may need to adjust the locations of the addressee's name, the page number and the date to keep the page balanced.

When you need to continue on another page, make sure you end the previous page appropriately.

- Avoid dividing a short paragraph (two or three lines). Move the entire paragraph to the next page.
- Divide a paragraph of four or more lines by leaving at least two lines at the bottom of the previous page.
- Do not divide the last word on a page.

Letters

TryOurAd Agency

115 Davis Parkway
White Plains, New York 10605
(914) 555-1234

December 1, 1994

Mr. Darren Hughes
Vice President
Executive Resources
212 Grand Avenue
Pinehurst, North Carolina 28374

Dear Mr. Hughes:

Please send me additional information about your conference facilities. We are planning a national sales meeting for 35 people in August 1995.

Since we want to combine some recreation along with our business meetings, let us know what choices we can select and what the extra charges are. A few members of the group are interested in fly fishing. Do you have stocked streams in the Pinehurst area in August?

We will be reviewing material from several sites in the next few weeks. Although price is always a consideration, we want to ensure that the site we choose contributes to the success of our meeting.

Sincerely,

Michelle Morrison

Michelle Morrison
National Sales Manager

MM:cs

Block Style

Letters

TryOurAd Agency
115 Davis Parkway
White Plains, New York 10605
(914) 555-1234

December 1, 1994

Mr. Darren Hughes
Vice President
Executive Resources
212 Grand Avenue
Pinehurst, North Carolina 28374

Dear Mr. Hughes:

Please send me additional information about your conference facilities. We are planning a national sales meeting for 35 people in August 1995.

Since we want to combine some recreation along with our business meetings, let us know what choices we can select and what the extra charges are. A few members of the group are interested in fly fishing. Do you have stocked streams in the Pinehurst area in August?

We will be reviewing material from several sites in the next few weeks. Although price is always a consideration, we want to ensure that the site we choose contributes to the success of our meeting.

Sincerely,

Michelle Morrison

Michelle Morrison
National Sales Manager

MM:cs

Modified Block Style

Business Style Guide

Letters

Related References

Information that appears in other chapters will help you with the following items:

complimentary closings	page	54
fonts	page	75
memos	page	108
salutations	page	143

Examples in This Chapter

To accommodate the size of this book, all of the examples in this chapter are shown at half their normal size. The proportions of the letter layouts are the same as if the examples appeared full size.

Lists

When used appropriately, lists can help your reader move quickly through a document. Used illogically or presented haphazardly, however, they can cause your reader to stumble.

Parallel Structure

When a list completes a thought begun in an introductory sentence, start each listed item with the same word form. Frequently, you will be using verbs to do this.

> As a result of the time management training program, I will:
> - prioritize my daily tasks.
> - write down my weekly goals.
> - delegate administrative tasks.

When you introduce a list with words such as *the following* or *as follows*, also make sure that each listed item has the same word form. Do not mix words ending in *ing* with words ending in *tion*, for example.

> Managers must cope with diverse responsibilities such as the following:
> - Delegating administrative tasks.
> - Preparing budgets.
> - Coordinating projects with other departments.

If you are using a vertical list of sentences, make sure each item in the series fits the definition of a sentence. Each sentence must have a subject and a verb, and it must express a complete thought.

> There were several benefits to attending the conference.
> - I had an opportunity to meet the competition.
> - Joe was able to give me advice within a minute of talking with customers.
> - Helping Joe assemble the portable booth gave me the hands-on experience I'll need when I take charge of the conference in California.

Bullets

Choose small bullets, not asterisks, dashes, hyphens, numbers or letters to highlight vertical lists. Bullets simply draw your reader's attention to another point; they do not indicate priority as numbers do or special significance as asterisks do.

Lists

Alignment

Align listed text evenly. Do not run text underneath the bullets or the space between the bullets and text. Use tabs, not the spacebar, to achieve alignment.

- Insert the customer's name in the field that is marked CUSTOMER. If there is no first name given, leave the space blank. If there are initials, use the initials without a space between them.

Use a dollar sign or percent sign only with the first amount in a vertical list. Right justify the numbers, or use a decimal tab. If the vertical column is summed, use a dollar sign or percent sign with the sum.

Here are the computer equipment expenditures we need to consider at tomorrow's meeting:

LAN server	$24,359.57	85.32%
Fax modem	438.95	1.54
Flat-bed scanner	1,095.75	3.84
Laser printer	2,655.00	9.30
	$28,549.27	100.00%

Upper or Lower Case

For vertical lists of phrases that complete an introductory sentence or come after the word *following*, you may use upper or lower case to start each item. When your list consists of complete sentences, however, always use upper case to start each sentence.

Punctuation

Always use a colon to introduce a list that comes after the expression *the following*. Either a period or a colon is acceptable in other cases.

Lists

Do not use a comma or semicolon after each listed item. Periods are necessary, however, for complete sentences and for items that finish an introductory statement. If the phrases that come after the word *following* are very short, periods are optional.

> Myrna is responsible for the following tasks:
> - typing letters
> - answering Mr. Maxwell's phone
> - responding to employment inquiries

When to List

A vertical list is a logical choice when you have three or more items to include. When you have only two items, try using a single sentence instead.

> Myrna is responsible for typing letters and answering Mr. Maxwell's phone.

Since readers need a combination of paragraphs and vertical lists to sense effective organization, limit your use of bulleted lists to no more than two per page.

Horizontal lists can be effective when you want to stress three or four short points in a single sentence. Use numbers in parentheses to accent each item.

> Myrna is responsible for: (1) typing letters, (2) answering Mr. Maxwell's phone, (3) responding to employment inquiries, and (4) scheduling interviews.

White Space

Indent vertical lists about a half inch to an inch from the left and right margins. When you surround lists with white space on both sides, you draw your reader's eyes to this section of your document. Refer to pages 156 and 157 for more information about using white space with a list of paragraphs.

Business Style Guide

me/myself/I

People who use *myself* incorrectly think they are being polite. There is nothing impolite about *me* or *I*, however.

Myself cannot be a substitute for *I* or *me*. When you have another person you are including with a reference to yourself, test for the appropriate word by deleting the other person.

> If you have any questions, please call Naomi or me.
>> That sentence is correct. You can tell it is by taking out *Naomi*: If you have any questions, please call me. You would not say: ... please call myself or ... please call I.
>
> After Harold and I reviewed the statistics, we agreed with everyone else's opinion.
>> That sentence is correct. You can tell it is by taking out *Harold*: After I reviewed the statistics .... You would not say: After me reviewed ... or After myself reviewed ....

The correct use of *myself* is to turn the action back on the subject or to emphasize that someone has acted alone. You must already have *I* in the sentence before you can use *myself*.

> I was able to correct the error myself.
>
> I will have no problem completing the project by myself.
>
> I prefer to do it myself.

The expression *between you and me* is a common one that raises questions. Is *me* correct? Yes. It's not correct to use *I* instead. Here's why: The word *me* always functions as an object, and the word *I* always functions as a subject. In the expression *between you and me*, the word *me* functions as the object of the preposition *between*.

107

Memos

Memos are for all correspondence within your organization. They belong on memo forms if they are available.

Required Items

The standard format at the top of a memo consists of four specific items.

>To:
>From:
>Date:
>Subject:

Sometimes the subject line is called a reference line and uses *Re:* or *Ref:* instead of the word *Subject*.

Memos do not have an inside address, salutation or closing as letters do. They end with the last line of your message.

Optional Items

Place your cc list on the third line below your last sentence unless your standard memo form has a place for it at the top.

Some people like to have their names typed a few lines below the last sentence. If you do that, you may also want to sign your name as you would in a letter.

Personalized Openings

To add a personal touch to the beginning of your memo, use the person's name in direct address, the way you would if you were speaking face-to-face. Either a comma or a colon is acceptable after the name. When you use a comma, you may continue your message on the same line or start a new line. If you use a colon, however, start your message on the next line.

>Helena, we need to meet this week to determine the final alterations required on Model 7W.
>
>Helena,
>We need to meet ....
>
>Helena:
>We need to meet ....

Memos

Alignment

Remember to use a tab, not the spacebar, to align the information vertically across from the four specific lines for *To, From, Date* and *Subject*. Leave one or two lines before you begin your message.

Left justify your message at the same margin as the words *To, From, Date* and *Subject*. Do not indent the entire message. The model on page 142 illustrates the correct format.

Related References

Information that appears in other chapters will help you with the following items:

complimentary closings	page 54
e-mail	page 66
fonts	page 75
letters	page 97
reference/subject lines	page 137

Memos

NUTRIFOODS
memorandum

To: Seth Ryan

From: Caroline Humphrey

Date: November 17, 1994

Re: *C-Bits* Packaging

We are on schedule for the final review of the new *C-Bits* back panel. Please check the enclosed proof to make sure we have accurately incorporated the changes you suggested.

Since Todd is meeting with the printer on Wednesday, I would like your OK by Tuesday morning at the latest.

I'll get back to you if the printer has difficulties setting some of your suggested layouts.

cc: Todd Minkas

Typical Memo Format.

Modifying Phrases

You may remember hearing the terms *misplaced modifier* or *dangling modifier*, but you may not remember what the terms mean. All modifying phrases should be next to the words they modify. When they are not, they are misplaced or dangling.

> After preparing the report, I checked with my colleagues to ensure that they agreed with my viewpoint.
>
> *After preparing the report* modifies *I*. Because the phrase starting with *After* is next to the word *I*, it is clear that I am the one who prepared the report.
>
> After reading the report, my colleagues agreed with me.
>
> *After reading the report* modifies *my colleagues*. They are the ones who read the report.
>
> After revising the data, the report was acceptable.
>
> That sentence is not correct because the report cannot revise the data. *After revising the data* is called a dangling modifier.
>
> To correct the sentence, you can clarify who revised the data: After we revised the data, the report was acceptable, or After revising the data, we found the report acceptable.

Where to Look for Mistakes

Most modifying problems occur at the beginning of sentences. If you check carefully every time you start a sentence with a qualifying group of words, you will catch most mistakes.

> As a valued customer, we would like to invite you to take advantage of extra savings on your next order.
>
> That sentence is not correct. Because the qualifying group of words, *As a valued customer*, comes right next to the word *we*, the meaning is that we are the valued customer.
>
> You can correct the sentence by including a word that identifies the valued customer: Since you are a valued customer, we would like to invite you to take advantage of extra savings on your next order.

Modifying Phrases

Problems with ing *and* ed *Endings*

Problem phrases often start with words that end in *ing* or *ed*. The problems occur in three situations:

- when *ing* or *ed* words are the first words in sentences.
- when *ing* or *ed* words follow words such as *when*, *after*, or *while*.
- when the word *in* or *by* comes before a word ending in *ing*.

If you spot any of these constructions, test the sentence by reading it with the subject first, and then insert the modifying phrase. If it is logical and correct, even though it may sound awkward, you will know that you do not have a dangling modifier.

> In establishing our objectives for next year, third quarter sales figures were an important part of our decision making.
>
>> That sentence is not correct. Note the word *In* followed by *establishing*. When you test the sentence by reading the subject first, here's the illogical construction you find: **Third quarter sales figures, in establishing our objectives for next year, were an important part of our decision making.**
>>
>> Third quarter sales figures cannot establish objectives. To correct the sentence, you can clarify who did the establishing: **In establishing our objectives for next year, we used third quarter sales figures as an important part of our decision making.**
>>
>> The test shows the correct logic this time: **We, in establishing our objectives for next year, used third quarter sales figures as an important part of our decision making.**
>
> When almost finished writing the six-page proposal, the system went down.
>
>> That sentence is not correct. Can the system write the proposal? When you test the sentence, you find this illogical construction: **The system, when almost finished writing the six-page proposal, went down.**
>>
>> To correct the sentence, you can clarify who was writing the proposal: **When I was almost finished writing the six-page proposal, the system went down.**

Modifying Phrases

Having a broken printer, the graphs will have to wait till tomorrow.

That sentence is not correct. Can the graphs have a broken printer? When you test the sentence, you find this illogical construction: The graphs, having a broken printer, will have to wait till tomorrow.

To correct the sentence, you can clarify who has the broken printer: Since we have a broken printer, the graphs will have to wait till tomorrow, or Having a broken printer, we will have to wait till tomorrow to print the graphs.

Other Problem Phrases

Other modifying problems can occur with phrases starting with words such as *about, with, from, on* or *in*. When these phrases are not next to the words they describe, they are considered misplaced modifiers.

The manager made a negative comment at a picnic about company policy.

That sentence is not correct. Does your company schedule picnics about company policy? *About company policy* is misplaced; it needs to be next to the word *comment*.

To correct the sentence, you can say: At a picnic, the manager made a negative comment about company policy, or The manager made a negative comment about company policy when he was at a picnic.

On a repetitive basis, I recommend you use our fold-out print ad to draw attention to your new product.

That sentence is not correct. What is *on a repetitive basis*? Because of its placement, the phrase *on a repetitive basis* must modify *I*, but that doesn't make sense. How can *I* be *on a repetitive basis*?

To correct the sentence, you can move the phrase next to the word *ad*: I recommend you use our fold-out print ad on a repetitive basis to draw attention to your new product. You also could say: To draw attention to your new product, I recommend you use our fold-out print ad on a repetitive basis.

none

If you learned that *none* always means "not one" and always takes a singular verb, you are not alone. Unfortunately, that general rule did not consider that *none* also means "not any." Like the words *some*, *most* and *all*, the word *none* can refer to something thought of as one unit. Or, it can refer to something thought of as a number of separate units.

> All of the information is accurate.
>
> All of the numbers are accurate.
>
> None of the information is accurate.
>
> None of the numbers are accurate.

To choose a verb that agrees with *none* when you mean "not any," check the *of* phrase immediately after *none*.

> **Since none of the customer service reps were available, I took care of the complaint.**
>
> > The subject is *none*. Since it refers to *reps*, which is plural, you need *were* as the verb.
>
> **None of the pizza was left.**
>
> > The subject is *none*. Since it refers to *pizza*, which is singular, you need *was* as the verb.

Keep in mind that this method of choosing verbs to agree with subjects is not typical. Most of the time you do not consider the *of* phrase. For more about subject–verb agreement, refer to pages 150 through 159.

When you want to emphasize the idea of *not one* or *no one*, use either of those terms rather than *none*.

> **Since no one in Customer Service was available, I took care of the complaint.**
>
> **Not one slice of pizza was left.**

Numbers

Because numbers are crucial in business documents, your primary goal needs to be ease of reading. As you review the rules, keep in mind that there will be times when you must use your own good judgment based on your audience and the nature of the document.

Spelling Out Numbers

Spell out numbers from one to ten.

> Feedback from seven managers will help us redesign the appraisal process.
>
> Please send us three copies of your proposal.

Always spell out numbers that begin a sentence. If necessary, rephrase the sentence to avoid starting with a figure, particularly when the figure refers to dollar amounts.

> Forty-seven orders were processed this week.
>> That sentence is correct. However, the number does not stand out as much as it does in the following sentence: **We processed 47 orders this week.**
>
> Three hundred fifty thousand dollars has been allocated for new equipment.
>> That sentence is correct. However, the number does not stand out as much as it does here: **Our allocation for new equipment is $350,000.**

Dollars and Percents

Use figures instead of words for dollar amounts and percents. This may require rephrasing sentences.

> The total project cost is $750,000.
>
> We experienced an 8% increase in profits this month.
>
> Our plan is to encourage 2% of the work force to take early retirement.
>> The number in that sentence would not stand out as much if you started the sentence with a word: **Two percent of the work force will be encouraged to take early retirement.**

115

Numbers

If you choose to use the word *percent*, spell out numbers from one to ten but use figures for any other numbers. In most business documents, using the symbol is an acceptable style, and you will not need to use the word *percent*.

> A seven percent decline in operating costs is expected early next year.
>
> A 7% decline in operating costs is expected early next year.
>
> Although only 27 percent of the people surveyed preferred the unscented product, we anticipate a more favorable response after the product is launched.
>
> Although only 27% of the people surveyed preferred the unscented product, we anticipate a more favorable response after the product is launched.

It is not necessary to add a decimal point and zeros to whole dollar amounts when they occur in sentences. It is necessary, however, when you choose to list a column of amounts.

> The average monthly account balance of $398,000 shows good control over cash flow.
>
>> Using a decimal point and two zeros would make it less clear for your reader: The average monthly account balance of $398,000.00 shows good control over cash flow. If your reader is skimming your document, he or she could mistake this number for $398,000,000.

Mixing Figures and Words

Avoid mixing figures and spelled-out numbers for similar items in the same sentence or paragraph. This does not hold true for mixing dollar amounts and figures relating to other items, however.

> My department has grown from three to sixteen in just two years. We are responsible for $20 million worth of business.
>
>> It is not necessary to write out *twenty million dollars* just because the numbers in the first sentence are words.

In a document such as an audit report, it's important to have dollar amounts and percentages stand out as figures while other items follow the rules consistent for spelling out numbers.

Numbers

MyCorp receives most of its cash via four lock box accounts maintained with four banks (annual throughput approximately $500 million). The lock box accounts receive cash directly from the customer or from any of the 17 branch locations. Sales representatives are required to receive cash from the customer on certain contract sales. Incentive plans exist for the rep to collect as much cash immediately as possible. This cash is then forwarded from the branch to the regional collection office's lock box account. Cash is also received in Jersey City (approximately $70 million annually) and is deposited daily in Jersey City Trust Bank.

> The number *four* needs to be spelled out because it is under ten. The number *17* does not need to be spelled out because it refers to an item completely different from a lock box account; it refers to branch locations. If there were other references to lock box accounts and the numbers were over ten, they would need to be spelled out to be consistent with references to similar items.

Our review of thirty annual contracts ($1.9 million) and fifty basic contracts ($1.6 million) disclosed several discrepancies regarding current approval policies. Sales management did not properly approve twelve annual contracts ($875,400) and five basic contracts ($778,000). Three basic contracts ($28,999) greater than $5,000 were not available for review although company policy requires contracts greater than $5,000 be sent to headquarters for approval. There was no evidence of proper approval for discounts on four annual and three basic contracts ($130,200).

> In that paragraph there are several references to contracts. The writer must decide whether to use figures consistently or to use words. Either style is acceptable as long as all references to the same item are consistent. Using words for contracts helps the dollar figures stand out.

Numbers

st, nd, rd *or* th

Avoid using figures with *st, nd, rd* or *th* except for centuries.

> The third time we contacted the disaster recovery unit, we received an immediate response. This should have been the case the first time, however.
>
>> *Third* and *first* are considered better style for business text. Using figures is not appropriate: The 3rd time that we contacted the disaster recovery unit, we received an immediate response. This should have been the case the 1st time, however.
>
> Our second quarter results show that new accounts are on the upswing.
>
>> If your department uses *1st, 2nd, 3rd* and *4th* as a routine style to refer to quarters, don't rock the boat. Your audience will see the figures as familiar but see the words as unfamiliar.
>
> Voice-activated computers will undoubtedly be popular in the 21st century.
>
>> The figure *21* is appropriate style; *the twenty-first century* is not necessary.

Hyphenating Compound Numbers

Hyphenate two-word numbers expressed as words, but not three-word numbers.

> Twenty-seven exhibitors have registered for next month's regional trade show.
>
> Three hundred fifty catalogs have printing mistakes that must be corrected.
>
>> Note that you do not use the word *and* between *hundred* and *fifty*.

Hyphenate two-word numbers when they are part of larger numbers.

> One hundred thirty-five million samples were sent via direct mail last week.

Business Style Guide

Numbers

Using Parentheses

You do not need duplicate references to one number unless your department has established this style as a way to double check amounts.

> The 23 reports we examined did not have any errors.
>> It is not necessary to use parentheses to clarify the number: The twenty-three (23) reports ....

Readability of Numbers in Text

To lower the risk of confusion for your reader, try to avoid more than four numbers in one sentence. If necessary, break a sentence into two or three separate ones. Also, avoid taking your reader through a calculation from beginning to end; start with the final number and then go back through the calculation.

> Our records indicate total premiums earned under this account are $32,574.72, and if we add the $10,570.30, which is a credit for the extra investment under contract B750, the total credited to Roberta Fulton's retirement account is $43,145.02.
>> Did you find that sentence confusing? Note the contrast in the following revision: The total credited to Roberta Fulton's retirement account is $43,145.02. Our records indicate total premiums earned under this account are $32,574.72 before adding the extra investment credit of $10,570.30 under contract B750.

More Information

Refer to page 104 for advice on listing numbers and page 62 for dates.

119

Open Punctuation

If you have seen letters that have no colon after the salutation and no comma after the complimentary closing, you can safely assume that the writer or organization has chosen to use open punctuation. While this style has not become very popular, some corporations have established it as part of their corporate identity on official letterhead.

Check with your corporate communications department before you decide to adopt this style. Since most people are not familiar with open punctuation, you risk having your reader think you forgot the colon and the comma.

Paragraphs

Creating effective paragraphs can give your writing extra power and keep your reader interested in your document. Each paragraph should focus on one idea or one point. However, deciding where to end one paragraph and start another is often a challenge. Although your decision is based primarily on content, keep in mind that your reader is influenced by the visual appearance of a document.

Ten Line Maximum

Limit a paragraph to a maximum of ten typed lines. If paragraphs are too long, you risk losing your reader. People who become impatient to get through a document may skip information buried at the end of a long paragraph. This principle is especially important for technical documents that are going to a nontechnical audience.

Variety

By varying paragraph lengths, you can provide an interesting landscape for your reader. Rather than strive for an average paragraph length, look at each document before you send it out and decide where you need some balance. For example, if one paragraph is seven lines, can you use just two or three lines in the next paragraph?

Breathing Space

Always double space between paragraphs. Think of giving your reader a chance to breathe before going on to the next point.

Paragraphs

One Liners

Avoid too many one-sentence paragraphs. Although your goal may be to simplify your message and encourage your reader, a page full of very short paragraphs (one or two lines each) looks unorganized. Everyone has learned that a paragraph is the basic unit for pulling ideas together under a central thought. If the document looks as though the ideas are not pulled together, the reader may not be motivated to read it.

Indenting

It's not necessary to indent the first line of each paragraph in any business document. Double spacing between paragraphs makes it clear to your reader that you have started a new paragraph. Newspapers and magazines have to use indented first lines, of course, because they do not have any extra space between paragraphs.

If you prefer the look of indented first lines, be careful how you place indented lists. Your document may not look as clear if you have indented first lines and other indented material.

White Space

Using white space to surround a list consisting of two or three paragraphs can draw extra attention to a particular section of a document. The example on the next page illustrates the visual impact you can create. (To fit the proportions of this book, this illustration is shown at half its normal size.)

Make sure this "double-indenting" technique is logical for the content you are presenting, and use headings to give your reader an overview of the items listed. Think of this group of paragraphs as a work of art framed with a wide mat to help the viewer/reader focus on content.

Paragraphs

Thanks for getting the revised contract to me so quickly. I have enclosed your signed copy along with the following marketing information:

Open Enrollment Seminars
Fifty presentation folders contain the latest open enrollment schedule and a brochure that gives you detailed information about us. I've also included a fax-ready copy of each of these brochures.

Executive Consultations
The large white envelope contains 10 brochures that explain these private coaching sessions. Please let your staff know that executive consultations are available in the New York Metro area only.

On-site Seminars
Ten presentation folders include brochures about our on-site seminars, including fees.

The confirmation package to each registrant includes a pre-course information sheet, our Business Writing Audit and directions to the seminar site.

We are eager to do all we can to make our new relationship a positive one. You can rely on us to provide all you need to help you communicate our services effectively.

White Space Surrounding a List of Paragraphs

Business Style Guide

Parallelism

To appreciate the value of parallel structure in writing, think about someone walking across a set of parallel bars when, all of a sudden, an outside force pulls one of the bars away from the other; the result is a mishap for the gymnast. Likewise, if your sentences and lists are not parallel, your readers are susceptible to being thrown off course. Writing that is not parallel causes readers to slow down because the words are not comfortable to the ear.

Parallel Sentences

When you join items or ideas in a sentence by using a connecting word (*and, but, or*), keep the words you are joining in the same form. For example, you may use all nouns, all adjectives, all gerunds (*ing* words), or all verb forms in the same tense.

> Microcomputers are compact, portable and inexpensive.
>> The three words describing microcomputers are all adjectives and therefore parallel in structure.
>
> An employee orientation program is worthwhile and necessary for success.
>> *Worthwhile* and *necessary* are both adjectives. If you had chosen the word *necessity* instead of *necessary*, the phrasing would not be parallel: An employee orientation program is worthwhile and a necessity for success.
>
> We are looking for engineers who can think logically, who can analyze carefully and who can make critical decisions quickly.
>> The parallel structure of *who can* plus a verb makes that sentence easy to follow.
>
>> You can also use a series of verbs without repeating *who can* for each group of words: We are looking for engineers who can think logically, analyze carefully and make critical decisions quickly. The words *who can think* start the structure that needs verbs to follow logically; your reader moves quickly through the sentence because of the rhythm created by *who can think, analyze and make.*

123

Parallelism

> If you have any questions or need further explanation, let me know.

That sentence is parallel because the verbs *have* and *need* follow logically after the subject *you*: If you have ... or need ....

> The following sentence would not be parallel, however: If there are any questions or the need for further explanation, let me know. *If there are the need* does not make sense and therefore is not parallel with *If there are any questions*.

Organizing and making long-range plans can help new managers deal effectively with project management.

> The words *organizing* and *making* are parallel because they both end in *ing*; they are gerunds. The following sentence would not be parallel: Organizing and long-range plans can help new managers deal effectively with project management.

Employees respect Mr. Grey but find him a little intimidating.

> That sentence is correct because *respect* and *find* are both verbs. The following sentence would not be parallel: Mr. Grey is a manager whom employees respect but is a little intimidating.

If you join ideas with *than*, also check for parallelism.

> Many small investors prefer to save their money than risk it.

Save and *risk* are both verbs in the present tense and therefore parallel. That sentence would not be parallel if you used the following construction: ... prefer to save their money than risking it.

Parallel Lists

Since lists are so popular in business, it's important to have them follow the same parallel structure that sentences require. When a list completes a thought begun in an introductory sentence, start each item with the same word form. Frequently, you will use verbs to do this.

> As a result of the time management training program, I will:
> - prioritize my daily tasks.
> - write down my weekly goals.
> - delegate administrative tasks.
>
> The verbs *prioritize*, *write* and *delegate* are parallel.

124

Business Style Guide

Parallelism

Myrna is responsible for: (1) typing letters, (2) answering Mr. Maxwell's phone, (3) responding to employment inquiries, and (4) scheduling interviews.

All four responsibilities start with words that end in *ing* (gerunds).

When you have a list of characteristics introduced by the word *following*, be careful to keep each item in the same form.

Managers must cope with diverse responsibilities such as the following:
- delegating administrative tasks
- preparing budgets
- coordinating projects with other departments

Since all three of the responsibilities start with words ending in *ing* (gerunds), the list is parallel. The following example is not parallel, however:

Managers must cope with diverse responsibilities such as the following:
- delegating administrative tasks
- budget preparation
- coordination of projects with other departments

If you are using a list of sentences, make sure each item in the series fits the definition of a sentence. The sentence must have a subject and a verb, and it must express a complete thought.

There were several benefits to attending the conference.

- I had an opportunity to meet the competition.
- Joe was able to give me advice within a minute of talking to customers.
- Helping Joe assemble the portable booth gave me the hands-on experience I'll need when I take charge of the conference in California.

Parenthesis

Use parentheses to set off explanatory material that your reader might not need but may find helpful. If your correspondence goes to a wide audience, it's possible that many of your readers do not need the information in parentheses but others do.

> Four of our clients (GCap, Wonderful Insurance, Trimark, and Beta Products) requested a simpler form.

> Based on the preliminary research, support is necessary in four offices in three of the largest cities in the country (Chicago, New York and Philadelphia), and we need to adjust our budget figures accordingly.

> The program will operate on a ten-month basis (September through June).

> The client plans to use a series of full-page ads in three publications for four months (August, September, October and November).

Problems with Parentheses

Avoid placing a full-sentence parenthetical comment in the middle of another sentence. This is especially important for technical material going to a non-technical audience. Place the parentheses at the end of the sentence, rephrase the sentence, or eliminate the parentheses.

> Creating an enhancement to the existing system (This would allow an additional batch job to be run at the end of each business week.) would free up the mainframe for greater access during the business day.
>
>> That sentence is not easy to read unless you are quite familiar with the systems terminology used. The revisions on the next page are much easier for all readers and will not bother systems professionals who are quite familiar with the material.
>
> Creating an enhancement to the existing system would free up the mainframe for greater access during the business day. (The enhancement would allow an additional batch job to be run at the end of each business week.)
>
> Creating an enhancement to the existing system would allow an additional batch job to be run at the end of each business week. This would free up the mainframe for greater access during the business day.

If the information in parentheses interrupts the flow of the sentence, rephrase the sentence.

Business Style Guide

Parenthesis

> We will be discussing relocation plans (specifically the attached ideas) at Friday's staff meeting.
>
>> That sentence is not as clear as the following revision: **We will be discussing the attached relocation plans at Friday's staff meeting.**
>
> September's figures (attached chart) indicate that our decision to consolidate two offices was the right move to make.
>
>> That sentence is not as clear as the following revision: **Note on the attached chart that September's figures indicate our decision to consolidate two offices was the right move to make.**

Punctuation with Parentheses

Do not add extra punctuation just because you are using parentheses. There is no need, for example, to have a comma before a parenthesis.

> **The mentor program instituted last month will have an impact on a large population (approximately 200).**
>
>> Using a comma after the word *population* would be incorrect even if the sentence continued after the parentheses.

Continue to use all the same punctuation the sentence would require if you were not putting information in parentheses. For example, use a period after the closing parenthesis when the information in parentheses ends a sentence. If the information in parentheses is a complete sentence, use a period just as you would if it were not inside the parentheses.

> **Our goal is to keep evaluation costs as low as possible (3% of budget or less).**
>
>> The period that ends the sentence goes outside the final parenthesis because it ends the entire sentence.
>
> **The marketing plan for the next three quarters includes the use of coupons distributed by mail. (Examples are on the attached list.)**
>
>> Since the information in parentheses is a complete sentence, you need a period before the final parenthesis. There is no need for a period after the final parenthesis because the sentence already ended after the word *mail*.

Prepositions

Traditional grammarians have given the advice never to end a sentence with a preposition such as *of, to, at, about, with* or *from*. Although this rule does not receive the same attention it once did, many people believe it is important. Decide what is best based on your audience and the document. In most cases, it's quite simple to rearrange the sentence to satisfy everyone.

> **The speaker had such a dynamic style that we found him very easy to listen to.**
>
>> That sentence is not going to bother most readers although it ends with a preposition. However, you can easily rephrase the sentence as follows: **The speaker had such a dynamic style that it was very easy to listen to him.**

In some cases, ending with a preposition gives a sentence more punch or makes it sound sincere. If you go out of your way to avoid the preposition at the end and create an awkward sentence, your readers are just as likely to react in a negative way.

> **If this is an example of the people you have working for you, you have much of which to be proud.**
>
>> That sentence is correct, but it sounds stilted. The following sentence sounds as though the writer is speaking: **If this is an example of the people you have working for you, you have much to be proud of.**

Winston Churchill, great orator and writer that he was, had perhaps the last word on this debate: All the discussion about ending sentences with prepositions was something, he said, "up with which I will not put!"

principal/principle

Use *principal* when you mean any of the following:

- chief or primary
- the head of a school or firm
- capital that earns or is charged interest

> The principal reason for hiring temps is to keep the workflow moving.
>
> The word you want means "chief" or "primary."

> One of the principals of the firm has experience with tax law.
>
> The word you want means "the head of a firm."

> The bank will charge 2% above the prime rate for a loan with a principal greater than $250,000.
>
> The word you want refers to "capital that is charged interest."

Use *principle* to refer to a rule or standard.

> The principles established here in the 1950s are still in place.
>
> The word you want means "rules" or "standards."

One way to remember the difference between these two words is to remember that both *principle* and *rule* end in *le*. Every time you're deciding which word you want, ask yourself, "Is this a rule?" If it is, you need *principle*. If it isn't, you need *principal*.

> The principal factor in our success is the staff's loyalty.
>
> If you asked yourself, "Is this a rule?" you would answer, "No."
> You need the word that does not end in *le* as *rule* does.

> The principles we have followed in the last ten years have stressed the involvement of everyone in the department.
>
> If you asked yourself, "Is this a rule?" you would answer, "Yes."
> You need the word that ends in *le* just as *rule* does.

Pronouns

Pronouns are words that take the place of nouns. Every pronoun must have another word it refers to (the antecedent) in the same sentence or the sentence immediately before.

> Our CEO has stressed that the new strategy he is implementing will produce results in the next quarter. It will not require further reduction in staff.

It refers to *strategy*, and *he* refers to *CEO*.

Rules for Agreement

When you use a singular pronoun (*he, she, it, this, his, her, anyone, its, everyone, each*), make sure that the word the pronoun refers to is also singular.

> Although the audit process has changed significantly, it still follows generally accepted accounting principles.

The pronoun *it* refers to *process*; both are singular.

When you use a plural pronoun (*they, these, them, their, we, us*), make sure that the word the pronoun refers to is also plural.

> Although the audit procedures have changed significantly, they still follow generally accepted accounting principles.

They refers to *procedures*; both words are plural.

Missing Antecedents

A common mistake is to use a pronoun such as *their, this, these, they* or *it* without an antecedent.

> Since we have received several calls about the manager's position that opened in our department last week, I have created a more detailed description of their responsibilities.

> The word *their* in the second part of the sentence does not have an antecedent. You need a noun, not a pronoun: ... I have created a more detailed description of the person's responsibilities.

> One advertising technique uses a creative photograph with almost no mention of the company's name; these are very popular in fashion magazines.

> The word *these* does not have an antecedent. There are two ways to correct the sentence: ... this technique is very popular ... or ... these photographs are very popular ....

Business Style Guide

Pronouns

Avoiding Sexist Writing

If you check a grammar book or style guide written before the '60s, the advice given would be to choose *his* or *he* when referring to one person. That advice is no longer accurate.

> When a person exercises every day, he is less likely to feel stressed or to have problems with his health.

>> That sentence would have been correct decades ago, but it is incorrect today. The writer cannot automatically assume that all the people exercising are male.

The best way to avoid sexist writing is to use the plural form.

> People who exercise every day are less likely to feel stressed or to have problems with their health.

>> The word *their* refers to *people*; both are plural.

> When managers must deal with a problem employee, they must remain calm and in control.

>> *They* refers to *managers*; both are plural.

The tendency in conversation is to use a plural pronoun to refer to a singular antecedent rather than suggest male or female only. Because you may hear these references often, you may think they are acceptable in writing. Your readers are more likely to notice the mistake in print, however.

> Anyone who has their degree can apply for the position.

>> That sentence is not correct because *their*, which is plural, cannot agree with *anyone*, which is singular. To correct the sentence, you can change *anyone* to a plural word: **People who have their degrees can apply for the position.** (Note that *degrees* must be plural also.)

Another way to avoid sexist writing is to use *a* or *the* instead of *his, her* or *their*.

> Anyone who has a degree can apply for the position.

>> The word *a* modifies *degree*; it is not a pronoun needing agreement with *anyone*.

> Someone has left a briefcase in the conference room.

>> Since there is no pronoun to refer to *someone*, sexist writing is not a problem in that sentence.

When you are writing directions or memos to a large distribution list, you can often avoid agreement problems by using the pronoun *you*.

Pronouns

> You are responsible for keeping your backup disk up to date.
>> If that sentence is in a memo directed to administrative assistants, each person will know that he or she is responsible.

Avoid using too many references that combine *his/her* or *he/she*.

> Each administrative assistant is responsible for keeping his/her backup disk up to date.
>> That sentence is nonsexist and correct, but if there are ongoing references to *his/her* and *he/she*, the writing will be awkward.

Avoid using *one* in place of a reference to male or female. Since people rarely use *one* in conversation, it sounds phony and distant on paper.

> One is responsible for keeping one's backup disk up to date.

Clarifying Antecedents

When a pronoun's antecedent is not clear, your reader may become confused.

> Jean Gladstone had a request from a sales representative for training materials that include good pointers for prospecting. Maria Capra referred her to us. I let her know you were out till Monday. In the meantime she is going to get more specific information.
>> Did the writer let Jean know or let Maria know? Is Jean getting more specific information, or is Maria? Because the pronouns *her* and *she* in the last two sentences are closer to *Maria*, it's possible that the reader could become confused. Correcting this potential problem simply requires putting in Jean's name one more time: I let Jean know ....

Possessive Pronouns

When pronouns indicate possession (ownership), they do not require apostrophes as nouns do. All of the following are possessive pronouns: *my, mine, our, ours, your, yours, his, her, hers, its, their, theirs* and *whose*.

More Information

The following pages answer questions about specific pronouns or their usage:

he/she/him/her	page 82
its/it's	page 95
me/myself/I	page 107
who/whom	page 165
whose/who's	page 166
you/your with *ing* words	page 167
your/you're	page 168

quicker/quickly

When you're choosing one of these words, remember that *quicker* must describe a person or thing and *quickly* describes how an action occurs. *Quicker* always implies a comparison.

> Version 6.1 of the software offers a quicker method to format documents.
>> The word *quicker* describes *method*. The implication is that there was an earlier version to compare to Version 6.1.
>
> The skills I learned in the seminar will help me to organize my thoughts quickly.
>> The word *quickly* describes how I will organize my thoughts. If you wanted to imply a comparison to an earlier experience, you would need to add the word *more*: The skills I learned in the seminar will help me to organize my thoughts more quickly.

Usually the word *quicker* comes before the word it describes. When that is not the case, the sentence will have a form of the verb *to be* (*is*, *are*, *was*, *were*, *be*, *being* or *been*). *Quickly* comes after the action it describes in most cases.

> This week's temporary administrative assistant is quicker at learning new skills than the person we had last week.
>
> This week's temporary administrative assistant learns new skills quickly.
>
> This week's temporary administrative assistant has learned new skills more quickly than last week's temp.

Quotation Marks

If your immediate reaction to quotation marks is that there are too many rules to remember, you probably had teachers who emphasized the rules for writing dialogue. Unless you are a professional editor who edits manuscripts, you can simplify the rules you need to know by focusing on the most common situations.

Someone's Exact Words

Use quotation marks to set off only the exact words said by someone.

> The business analyst said Quick Pro is "in an excellent position for growth in the '90s."
>
>> The words enclosed in quotation marks are the exact words the analyst used.

Do not use quotation marks if you do not use the exact words. When you use the words *said that*, you probably do not need quotation marks.

> Mary Ann said that she was going to send us form BAT50 by the end of the week.
>
>> That sentence does not provide the exact words Mary Ann used.
>
> Rodney told me that he would not be available for special projects next year.
>
>> Although Rodney might have used the words *available* or *special projects* or even *next year*, that sentence does not give the exact wording Rodney used.
>
>> If the sentence quoted Rodney exactly, it would have Rodney talking about himself: **Rodney said, "I will not be available for special projects next year."**

Most business correspondence does not require the use of quotation marks to refer to what someone says. You are more likely to paraphrase information and therefore use the words *said that*. However, when you need to document problems with people or respond to complaints, you may find it valuable to give your readers the exact words someone used.

> Your request to "schedule more animated meetings" may be difficult to implement.
>
>> The writer, who is undoubtedly responding to a complaint, may want people on the cc list to know the exact words used by the person he or she is addressing.
>
> When I spoke with Hank about his lateness, he responded, "I always get my work done. That's more than you can say about Oliver!"
>
>> The writer, who is undoubtedly documenting a discussion about a problem, probably wants the reader to know Hank's exact words because they convey a specific attitude.

Business Style Guide

Quotation Marks

Special Interpretations

When you want words to stand out as having a special meaning, use quotation marks around them.

> If we move our back office operations to Long Island, everyone will have to cope with the "world's longest parking lot."
>> The writer is not referring to a parking lot at all. The quotation marks tell you that the expression has a special meaning. Readers who are familiar with it will quickly recognize that people will have to cope with the Long Island Expressway, a highway known for so much volume that people are often sitting (almost parked!) in traffic delays.

Although sarcasm is risky in business documents, you may need to use quotation marks when you have a sarcastic meaning for something that is usually a typical phrase.

> Beatrice has been assigned yet another "priority task."
>> The sarcasm may have to do with the assignment of so many tasks that they can't all be priorities.

No Quotes Necessary

A common mistake is to use quotation marks around phrases that do not need them.

> Now that we have a task force working on the project, we can expect to see some progress soon.
>> There is no need to use quotation marks around a term such as *task force*.

> Since the WonderButter Research Project is on target, R&D does not anticipate delays in the planned product launch date of June 15.
>> There is no need to use quotation marks around a capitalized title such as *WonderButter Research Project*.

Commas and Periods

You need a comma before the quotation only when the material you are quoting follows a word such as *said, commented, concluded, responded, replied, answered* or *stated*.

> When I asked the angry customer what I could do to make a difference, he replied, "Nothing would make me change my mind!"
>> Note that you also use a capital letter to start the quoted material when you introduce the quote with a word such as *replied*.

Quotation Marks

Place the final quotation marks after commas and periods. This is American style, not British style.

> The CEO instructed all regional vice presidents to tell the staff there is "absolutely no basis for these rumors."

Note that this rule applies if the whole sentence is quoted material or if just a few words are quoted at the end of the sentence.

Rules You Rarely Need

Quotation marks are appropriate for titles of articles or chapter titles in a book.

> The article I read in *Business Week*, "Measuring the Total in Total Quality," suggested that service organizations have difficulty quantifying results.

Closing quotation marks go before colons and semicolons.

> The article I read in *Business Week* was "Measuring the Total in Total Quality"; it suggested that service organizations have difficulty quantifying results.

Closing quotation marks go after question marks when the quoted material includes a question.

> Several people in the meeting asked, "When can we expect to upgrade our equipment?"

Place closing quotation marks before question marks when the question has to do with the whole sentence, not just the quoted material.

> Did he actually say, "You're incompetent"?

Use only one question mark to end a sentence when the entire sentence and the quoted material are questions.

> Do you always ask, "What's in it for me?"

For exclamation points, follow the same rules given for question marks.

Single quotation marks are necessary only when you have a quote within another quote.

> My manager responded, "Your office reminds me of the famous expression 'empty desks suggest empty heads.'"

Reference/Subject Lines

A reference line in either a memo or letter can help your reader decide on the priority of the document.

>Re: Update on the Munroe Account
>>If the Munroe account is especially important, that line will draw your reader's attention. If the account is not as important as other subjects, your reader will probably delay reading your message.

Are Reference Lines Required?

All memos must have a reference or subject line, but in letters, the choice is yours. If you don't feel you need one, by all means, don't clutter your letter with an unnecessary line. If it can save time for your reader, however, include one.

Placement and Format

In memos, the standard format makes it easy to place a reference line.

>To:
>From:
>Date:
>Re:

The reference line may be noted in any of the following ways:

>Re:
>RE:
>Ref:
>Reference:
>Subject:

Note that each word is followed by a colon. Use a tab, not the spacebar, to align all of the items vertically across from the words *To, From, Date* and *Re.* The model memo on page 110 illustrates this alignment.

In letters, reference lines come between the inside address and the salutation. The preferred form is to left-justify no matter what letter format you use.

137

Reference/Subject Lines

> Mr. Thomas Financier
> Executive Vice President
> The Greatest Banking Company
> 1234 West GBC Plaza
> Schaumburg, IL 60168
>
> Re: Expansion of Mutual Funds Market
>
> Dear Mr. Financier:

If you learned that reference lines belong below the salutation, keep in mind that business letters have become more personalized in the last two decades. Having a reference line after the salutation breaks up your greeting.

People used to underline reference lines to make them stand out. There is no need to do that, however. Nor is there any need to put them in italics, boldface or all upper case.

Content

Make your reference line as specific as you can without creating a complete sentence. To avoid boring your reader, do not use the very same wording as the first line of your letter or memo. In most cases, your subject line helps you get to the point in your opening paragraph.

> Your Questions about Invoicing
>> That line gets your reader involved immediately. When you are responding to someone's question, it is a logical style to use.
>
> Schedule for System Enhancements
>> That line will encourage your readers to pull out their calendars as they are reading.

Reference/Subject Lines

Networking Problems
> Although no one likes to hear bad news, a line announcing problems can be very effective when the people receiving the message are the ones responsible for solving problems.

Your April 7 Letter
> That line helps you avoid an opening line that says you received the reader's letter.

Policy #7893270
> A line that gives a specific account number makes it easy for the reader to refer to the appropriate file.

E-Mail

Unless your readers are relying on filters to help them decide which messages to read, they must rely on your subject line. Keep in mind that your subject line competes with a mailbox full of subject lines. Consequently, the more specific you are, the more you can convince your reader to read your message.

Some companies have adopted the style of beginning e-mail subject lines with verbs. If you are the one giving the directive, this style may seem logical. However, if you're on the receiving end, it may be daunting to have a mailbox full of commands. Usually, key words will be sufficient.

Two Lines: Reference and Subject

Some organizations have a standard memo format that has a place for both a reference and a subject. In this case, reserve the reference line for dates of other relevant documents, file numbers, order numbers or other numerical references.

```
Subject:     Specifications for Monorail Construction
Reference:   Bid #321A
```

Run-on Sentences

Run-on sentences are not just long sentences. They are mistakes caused by combining two complete thoughts incorrectly. Some people call this error a comma fault or a comma splice because the writer uses a comma to separate the complete thoughts.

Most run-on sentences occur because writers do not take time to proofread carefully. This is especially true in e-mail messages when people are in a hurry.

Some run-on sentences occur because people do not see where one complete thought ends and another complete thought begins. If this is true for you, try reading sentences aloud to help you catch mistakes.

> Our meeting scheduled for Thursday is in Room 3A, the speaker will be representing the State Department.
>> That sentence is not correct. It is a run-on sentence because it does not end after *Room 3A*.
>
> Our meeting scheduled for Thursday is in Room 3A.
>> That is a complete sentence. The subject is *meeting* and the verb is *is*.
>
> The speaker will be representing the State Department.
>> That is a complete sentence. The subject is *speaker* and the verb is *will be representing*.

Two Sentences, Not One

The easiest way to correct a run-on sentence is to create two sentences.

> Thank you for meeting with Travis and me, we hope our presentation explained the benefits of advertising with us.
>> That sentence is not correct. It is a run-on sentence because it does not end after the word *me*. To correct the error, you need to create two sentences: **Thank you for meeting with Travis and me. We hope our presentation explained the benefits of advertising with us.**
>
> This package should give you everything you need for your long-range planning, I'll be sure to call next week to answer any questions.
>> That sentence is not correct. It is a run-on sentence because it does not end after the word *planning*. To correct the error, you need to create two sentences: **This package should give you everything you need for your long-range planning. I'll be sure to call next week to answer any questions.**

Business Style Guide

Run-on Sentences

However, Therefore and Also

Watch out for the words *however, therefore* and *also*. These words can start new sentences, but you cannot use them along with commas to connect complete thoughts.

> Shannon recommended that we hire a temporary to help us catch up on the database changes, therefore, we could have the changes complete by December 1.
>> That sentence is not correct. You can eliminate the run-on by creating two sentences: **Shannon recommended that we hire a temporary to help us catch up on the database changes. Therefore, we could have the changes complete by December 1.**
>
> The mailing was scheduled to go out last week. However, the brochure arrived at the mailing house a week late because of a printing delay.
>> Those two sentences are correct. The following is a run-on sentence because the complete thoughts are connected by *however* and commas: **The mailing was scheduled to go out last week, however, the brochure arrived at the mailing house a week late because of a printing delay.**

Refer to page 87 for more information about the use of *however*.

Changing Relationships

Sometimes the best way to correct a run-on sentence is to change the relationship of the ideas you are expressing.

> I was too tired to complete the work, therefore, I went home at 6:30.
>> That run-on sentence could be corrected as follows: **Since I was too tired to complete the work, I went home at 6:30.**
>
> We have increased production this quarter, therefore, we need to increase sales.
>> That run-on sentence could be corrected as follows: **Since we have increased production this quarter, we need to increase sales.**

Run-on Sentences

Semicolons, or **And** *and* **But**

You can use a semicolon to correct a run-on sentence as long as the two complete thoughts you are separating are very closely related.

> The project is not costly; however, it will take several weeks to complete.
>> That sentence is correct. Because both thoughts are closely related, using a semicolon is acceptable. Remember that you must have a subject and verb and express a complete thought on each side of the semicolon.

You can also correct a run-on sentence by inserting either *and* or *but* as long as it is logical to combine the ideas with those words.

> The project is not costly, but it will take several weeks to complete.
>> That sentence is correct.

Business Style Guide

Salutations

Salutations are appropriate only for letters, not for memos or e-mail messages. The standard form uses the word *Dear* followed by a title (*Dr.*, *Mr.*, *Ms.*, *Mrs.*), the person's last name and a colon.

>Dear Mr. Troyanos:

>Dear Ms. Latham:

If you want to personalize a memo or an e-mail message, use only the reader's name, not the word *Dear*. For details about punctuation and placement, refer to page 108 (Memos) or to page 66 (E-mail).

First Name Only

When you use a person's first name instead of a title and a last name, you indicate that you have some relationship already established with the person. You probably have spoken with him or her on the phone if you have not met in person.

You still need a colon after the name. Do not use a comma for business correspondence; reserve that for personal letters.

>Dear Jim:

>Dear Elisha:

Initials but No First Name

When you don't know whether the person you are writing to is male or female and you have only initials, include the initials but leave out *Mr.* or *Ms.*

>Dear J. W. Arnott:

Another choice, of course, is to call the individual's organization to find out if you need *Mr.* or *Ms.* Or, ask someone in your organization who knows your reader.

If you are creating a merged letter using database or word processing software, the letter's data record has a field for the addressee's title. Although merged letters can be designed to omit this field for specific records, you may have to talk with someone in your systems department to accomplish that task.

Distinguishing Male and Female Names

When you don't know the person and you have a name that could be either male or female, do not assume that the individual is a man. Depending on the purpose of your letter, it may be worth your trouble to find out from someone else in your organization, or even to make a phone call to your reader's organization, to clarify whether you need *Mr.* or *Ms.*

Salutations

If it is not feasible for you to find out, use the person's first and last name and omit *Mr.* or *Ms.*

Dear Terry Brockton:

Dear Darrell Morrison:

Merged letter software permits substituting the person's first name for the title if this situation arises. You don't want to insult your reader just because your computer says you have to.

No Name Given

If you don't have the name of the person who will be receiving your letter, do not use any of the antique expressions such as *Dear Sir, Dear Sirs, Dear Sir/Madam, Dear Ladies and Gentlemen, Gentlemen* or the highly impersonal *To Whom it May Concern.* There are three options that are more appropriate for business at the end of the 20th century.

Option One: Call the organization and get a name. If you're hoping to do business with someone, this should be your choice.

Option Two: Change the format of your letter to omit the salutation. After the inside address, leave two blank lines and begin the text of your letter. The example on the next page illustrates this style.

> Accounts Receivable
> Trittico Corporation
> 111 Sepulveda Boulevard
> Los Angeles, CA 90049
>
> To process your invoice #575, we need your current Federal Identification Number.

Salutations

Your letter will look balanced as long as you omit the complimentary closing. When you get to the end of the text of your letter, leave four blank lines and type your name and title. Sign your name above your typed name.

> If you have any questions, please call me.
>
> *Michael Feldman*
>
> Michael Feldman
> Manager of Finance

Option Three: Use an appropriate job title. This is the style used in a lot of direct mail letters. While it is impersonal, at least it does not offend anyone.

>Dear Human Resources Professional:
>
>Dear Training Director:
>
>Dear Audit Manager:

Ms., Mrs. or Miss

You are always correct in using *Ms.* to address women in business. Despite its rocky start in the '60s, this title is well established in the business community and does not separate women according to their marital status.

If you know that the person you are addressing prefers to be called *Mrs.*, you should use that title. Women who want to be addressed as *Mrs.* instead of *Ms.* have an obligation to let others know that by signing their names with *Mrs.* in all their own correspondence.

Salutations

Dr.

When it is appropriate to use the title *Dr.* in your salutation for either a Ph.D. or a medical doctor, be sure to double check your inside address for the correct style.

Inside Address	Salutation
Dr. Raymond Yin	Dear Dr. Yin:
Raymond Yin, M.D.	Dear Dr. Yin:

Do not use *Mr.* with *M.D.* in the inside address.

Dr. Grace Orlofsky	Dear Dr. Orlofsky:

Do not use *Ms.* or *Ph.D.* in the inside address.

If you have only initials, there is no dilemma about using *Mr.* or *Ms.*

M. L. Birnbaum, M.D.	Dear Dr. Birnbaum:

Esq.

Although *Esq.* is commonly used after an attorney's name in the inside address, there is no special title to use in the salutation.

Inside Address	Salutation
Steven G. Harvey, Esq.	Dear Mr. Harvey:

Do not use *Mr.* with *Esq.* in the inside address.

According to most dictionaries, the word *esquire* is considered a title of respect after a man's last name. Despite the origin of the word, however, it is acceptable in the United States to use it also for women who are attorneys.

Semicolon

The most common use of a semicolon is to combine two very closely related ideas that can stand alone as separate sentences.

> Managing five accounts is easy; managing fifty accounts is impossible.
>
> Customer Service uses quarterly phone calls to survey the level of customer satisfaction; however, the statistics may not be valid for every region.
>
> Brand loyalty is our goal; brand dilution is not.
>
> The project has been extended two more months; it began in July.

Horizontal Lists

Use a semicolon instead of a comma to separate horizontally listed items that already have commas within them.

> We have regional offices in Atlanta, Georgia; Denver, Colorado; Dallas, Texas and Bakersfield, California.
>
>> Without semicolons, your reader would have trouble distinguishing each unit made up of a city and a state. Note that a semicolon after *Dallas, Texas* is optional.

Misuse of Semicolons

Do not use a semicolon at the end of each item in a vertical list. Although you may see this style in legal documents, it is not necessary in business documents such as letters, memos, reports and proposals.

> We have established three methods of accurately tracking bugs in the system:
> - Phone calls from users are the most reliable sources because we can gain the most information.
> - E-mail messages give us a "quick and dirty" view.
> - The help desk keeps a log of questions from users.

Do not use a semicolon interchangeably with a colon. Semicolons are not appropriate to introduce lists, for example.

> The following goals will be the basis for our diversity program next year:
>
>> The use of a colon after a sentence with the word *following* is correct; a semicolon would be incorrect.

Avoid using a semicolon to create a sentence that is longer than 30 words (about three lines). Your readers need the visual break of a new sentence to encourage them to keep reading.

Sentence Length

A good average sentence length for business is in the range of 14 to 20 words. With this average, you may have some 30-word sentences as well as sentences with only 10 words. On this page the average sentence length is 16.

Most style checkers available on personal computers will calculate an average sentence length for you. If you want to get an estimate without using software, you can generally estimate 10 words for every line.

Balancing Short and Long

If you have to use long sentences, try to balance them by using short sentences close by. This is especially important if you are communicating technical information to a nontechnical reader.

Readability studies show that people can quickly comprehend a 20-word sentence and move on to the next thought. A 30-word sentence causes them to slow down, however, and a 40-word sentence may require rereading.

Limiting Short Sentences

The shorter the sentence, the greater the emphasis. That's true as long as all of your sentences are not too short. If your average sentence length is below 10, for example, there may not be an opportunity for any one sentence to stand out.

Avoid using too many short sentences in a row; you can easily create a choppy style that your reader may find condescending.

Split Infinitives

An infinitive is made up of the word *to* plus a verb. When you split an infinitive, you insert a word between *to* and the verb: *to review* is an infinitive; *to carefully review* is a split infinitive.

In the majority of cases, it is wise to avoid splitting infinitives because they sound awkward.

> **My manager had to frequently meet with the new research team to keep the project focused.**
>
> The split infinitive, *to frequently meet*, does not sound right to most ears. As a result, the reader is likely to slow down and pay more attention to the words than to the overall message.
>
> The sentence can be more effective without a split infinitive: **My manager had to meet frequently with the new research team ....** Or, **My manager had to meet with the new research team frequently ....**
>
> **Charlotte has trouble when she needs to quickly make a decision.**
>
> The split infinitive, *to quickly make*, detracts from the meaning more than it adds to the meaning. That sentence can be more effective without a split infinitive: **Charlotte has trouble when she needs to make a decision quickly.**

On rare occasions, a split infinitive can help you emphasize a particular word and therefore add to the effectiveness of your message.

> **As a result of the fire, the company had to completely rebuild its research facility.**
>
> The split infinitive, *to completely rebuild*, adds to the emphasis of major work ahead. The connotation is that the building burned to the ground. The sentence would not be as effective without the split infinitive: **As a result of the fire, the company had to rebuild its research facility completely.**

Subject-Verb Agreement

A singular subject must have a singular verb; a plural subject must have a plural verb. If you do not choose the right verb to agree with a subject, your reader may "hear" the mistake and lose your message.

> The meeting of the sales representatives is on Tuesday.
>
> *Is* agrees with *meeting*.
>
> The meetings we have scheduled for first quarter are all on Fridays.
>
> *Meetings* and *are* agree.

As long as the subject and verb are close together, you will probably not make mistakes. Business sentences, however, often require several words between the subject and the verb.

The key to avoiding errors is to make sure you have correctly identified the subject.

Prepositional Phrases

The subject will never be in phrases that begin with the words *in, at, of, for, to* or *with*. These phrases are called prepositional phrases.

> Changes in the new accounting system are simplifying year-end procedures.
>
> *Changes* is the subject, not *accounting system*. The phrase *in the new accounting system* is a prepositional phrase. The verb *are* agrees with the plural subject *changes*.
>
> New technology in international communication and computers is dictating change in work hours, travel and routine.
>
> *Technology* is the subject, not *communication and computers*. The phrase *in international communication and computers* is a prepositional phrase. The verb *is* agrees with the singular subject *technology*.
>
> Consideration for eligibility and financial assistance is dependent on three years of financial statements.
>
> *Consideration* is the subject, not *eligibility and financial assistance*. The phrase *for eligibility and financial assistance* is a prepositional phrase. The verb *is* agrees with *consideration*.

Subject–Verb Agreement

Part of the reason for substantially streamlining our operations is to control costs.

> *Part* is the subject, not *streamlining* or *operations*. The phrase *for streamlining our operations* is a prepositional phrase. The verb *is* agrees with *part*.

All members of the PAD committee are to meet next Thursday at 10:00.

> *Members* is the subject, not *committee*. The phrase *of the PAD committee* is a prepositional phrase. The verb *are* agrees with *members*.

The analysis of the data in the JKL system shows that we have improved our turnaround time.

> *Analysis* is the subject, not *data* or *system*. The phrases *of the data* and *in the JKL system* are prepositional phrases. The verb *shows* agrees with the singular subject *analysis*.

There

Beware of sentences beginning with *There*. Although it will seem that *There* is the subject, the real subject will appear later in the sentence.

There are five candidates who meet our requirements.

> The word *candidates* is the subject. The verb *are* agrees with it because *candidates* is plural. You can turn the sentence around to test this: **Five candidates who meet our requirements are there.**

There are two 15-minute meetings scheduled to review the procedures and to answer any questions.

> The word *meetings* is the subject. The verb *are* agrees with it. Remember your turnaround test: **Two 15-minute meetings are scheduled to review the procedures and to answer any questions.**

There are quarterly customer service evaluations scheduled to keep everyone informed.

> The subject is the word *evaluations*. The verb *are* agrees with it. Here's your turnaround test: **Quarterly customer service evaluations are scheduled to keep everyone informed.**

Subject–Verb Agreement

> There are several opportunities for advancement in this area.
>> The subject is *opportunities*. The verb *are* agrees with it. Your turnaround test proves that *are* is the correct verb: **Several opportunities for advancement are there.**

A common mistake in speaking is to use the contraction *there's* with a plural subject.

> There's several opportunities for advancement in this area.
>> That sentence is not correct. Since *opportunities* is the subject, the contraction for *there is* will not fit.

Enclosed *and* The Following

Double check sentences beginning with *Enclosed is/are* or *The following is/are*. The word *enclosed* is never the subject. Just as with the word *there*, you need to find the subject later in the sentence. When you use *The following*, you must look for the word that *following* refers to. If that word is plural, you need *are*; if it is singular, you need *is*.

> Enclosed are the brochures you requested.
>> The word *brochures* is the subject. The verb *are enclosed* agrees with it.

> The following is the information we compiled as a result of three focus groups:
>> The subject is *information*. The verb *is* agrees with it because *information* is singular.

> The following are my thoughts on the key issues you raised yesterday.
>> The subject is the word *thoughts*. The verb *are* agrees with it.

Is, Are, Was, Were, Has *and* Have

Most subject–verb errors in business occur with the verbs *is, are, was, were, has* and *have*. Double check when you use these verbs to make sure you have identified the subject correctly.

> The order of stationery supplies was delayed by three days.
>> The subject is *order*. The verb *was delayed* agrees with it because *order* is singular. Note the prepositional phrase *of stationery supplies*; remember the subject is never in a prepositional phrase.

Business Style Guide

Subject–Verb Agreement

Our competition in the northeastern and central markets is especially fierce.

> The subject is *competition*. The verb *is* agrees with it because *competition* is singular. Did you notice the prepositional phrase *in the northeastern and central markets*?

New packaging of the products with consumer criteria in mind is our next responsibility.

> *Packaging* is the subject. The verb *is* agrees with it because *packaging* is singular. Note that you have three prepositional phrases between the subject and the verb: *of the products*, *with consumer criteria* and *in mind*.

Revised plans for rebuilding the fifty-year-old conference center were reviewed in yesterday's meeting.

> The subject is *plans*. The verb *were reviewed* agrees with it because the word *plans* is plural. Note the long prepositional phrase: *for rebuilding the fifty-year-old conference center*.

The associates in Harold's department are assured of receiving good coaching in customer service skills.

> The subject is *associates*. The verb *are assured* agrees with it because *associates* is plural.

The implementation of two new reconciliation programs has simplified our month-end procedures.

> The subject is *implementation*. The verb *has simplified* agrees with it.

Anyone, Each, One *and* Everyone

Check for pronouns such as *anyone, each, one* or *everyone* that refer to one, not more than one. When any of these words function as the subject, you need to make sure you use a singular verb.

Each of the vice presidents has five minutes to speak.

> The subject is *each*. The verb *has* agrees with it because *each* is singular. The words *vice presidents* cannot be the subject because they occur in the prepositional phrase starting with *of*.

153

Subject–Verb Agreement

Each of you is responsible for following these new procedures accurately on September 18.
> *Each* is the subject. The verb *is* agrees with it because *each* is singular.

Each of the candidates we are looking at has outstanding credentials.
> *Each* is the subject. The verb *has* agrees with it.

One of the goals of the new evaluation methods is to maintain the same statistical base for all programs.
> *One* is the subject. The verb *is* agrees with it because *one* is singular. Did you notice the two interrupting prepositional phrases?

One of the key issues, of course, is how much the new system will cost.
> *One* is the subject. The verb *is* agrees with it because *one* is singular.

Everyone we plan to interview has a master's degree.
> *Everyone* is the subject. The verb *has* agrees with it because *everyone* is singular.

Anyone who wants to apply for the position is advised to submit an application before November 1.
> *Anyone* is the subject. The verb *is advised* agrees with it because *anyone* is singular.

Two Subjects, One Verb

When the subject has two or more parts joined by *and*, you need a plural verb.

The technology and the personnel in charge are the major considerations.
> The subject consists of two items: *technology* and *personnel*. The verb *are* agrees because the subject is plural.

Subject–Verb Agreement

Or and Nor

When you use *or* or *nor*, the verb must agree with the part of the subject closest to the verb.

> Neither the business analyst nor the investors were aware of the implications.
>> The verb *were* agrees with *investors* because that is the word closest to the verb.

> Neither the investors nor the business analyst was aware of the implications.
>> The verb *was* agrees with *analyst* because that is the word closest to the verb.

As Well As, But Not and Other Interrupters

Some subjects that appear to be plural are actually singular. Similarly, some subjects that appear to be singular are actually plural. Double check your agreement if you include an interrupting phrase that starts with any of the following: *as well as, together with, along with, but not, in addition to.*

> The design of the program, as well as its benefits for end users, was evident in the proposal.
>> The subject is *design*, and the verb *was* agrees with it. The phrase *as well as its benefits for end users* is not considered in determining the subject.

> The trains, but not the ferry, were running on time today.
>> The subject is *trains*, and the verb *were* agrees with it. The phrase *but not the ferry* is not considered in determining the subject.

> Zyad's training department, together with the community college, has scheduled a series of workshops called Parenting Skills for Working Parents.
>> The subject is *training department*, and the verb *has scheduled* agrees with it. The phrase *together with* is not considered in determining the subject.

Refer to page 31 for more information about the phrase *as well as*.

Subject–Verb Agreement

Team, Committee *and* Group

When you use *team, committee* or *group* to refer to one unit, use a singular verb. This is American style, not British style.

> The research team is meeting on Friday.
>> Everyone knows that more than one person is on the team, but the word *team* functions as one unit.

> The committee in charge of the revision is scheduled to complete its work by April 1.
>> Everyone knows that more than one person is on the committee, but the word *committee* functions as one unit.

> The committee in charge of selecting convention sites for the next three years has focused primarily on costs.
>> Since the word *committee* functions as one unit, the verb *has* is the verb that agrees.

> The group requesting a product review is concerned with packaging.
>> There are several people who make up the group, but the word *group* refers to one unit.

Data

In most business areas, *data* has become a singular noun meaning "a mass of information."

> The data supporting our decision is based on three years of product testing.
>> *Data* used as a singular noun requires the singular verb *is*.

If you work in a research environment, however, you are probably accustomed to seeing *data* as the plural form of *datum*. To you, *data* means "pieces of information," and you want a plural verb.

> When the emissions data were collected, no one knew the impact they would have on the ozone depletion studies.
>> *Data* used as a plural noun requires the plural verb *were collected*.

Subject–Verb Agreement

Number *and* Variety

Use a plural verb for *number* and *variety* when *a* comes before either of these words.

> A number of people have asked the same question.

> A variety of alternatives were considered.

Use a singular verb for *number* and *variety* when you have *the* before these words.

> The number of cases considered was 27.

> The variety of products presented at this year's exposition was astounding.

Total

Use a plural verb for *total* when *a* comes before it.

> A total of seven customers are attending the conference.

The only exception to this rule occurs with dollar amounts. When you use the word *total* with an expression of money, use a singular verb. Also use a singular verb when the dollar amount is the subject.

> A total of $20,000 was collected for the fund.

> Five hundred dollars was collected from our department to assist the victims of the fire.

When *the* comes before *total,* use a singular verb.

> The total collected was $20,000.

> The total enrollment was below last year's.

Subject–Verb Agreement

None

The word *none* sometimes requires a plural verb. Refer to page 114 for an explanation of this unusual case.

Two Verbs, One Subject

When you have two verbs referring to one subject, make sure that both verbs agree.

> The plan to streamline our operations is underway and is well accepted by the staff.
>> Both of the verbs *is* agree with the subject *plan*.

> The original contract for each client is filed in the regional office and is categorized as renewable or nonrenewable.
>> The verbs *is filed* and *is categorized* agree with the singular subject *contract*.

Subordinate Clauses

The most challenging situation for subject–verb agreement occurs with subordinate clauses. These are groups of words that have a subject and a verb, but they cannot stand alone as complete thoughts.

Typical subordinate clauses begin with *that, which, since, when, after, although,* and *because*. The subject and verb in the subordinate clause must agree with each other just as the subject and verb in the main clause do.

> Since the new plan enables us to process applications more quickly, we need to begin using it immediately.
>> The subordinate clause starts with *Since* and ends with *quickly*; the subject in the clause is *plan*, and the verb *enables* agrees with it. The main clause starts with *we* and ends the sentence; the subject is *we*, and the verb *need* agrees with it.

> Ted reported that plans for our fall meeting in Phoenix are well underway.
>> The main clause is *Ted reported*. The subordinate clause beginning with *that* has *plans* as the subject and *are* as the verb.

Subject–Verb Agreement

Sometimes a subordinate clause separates the subject and verb of the main clause. The two typical words to watch out for are *that* and *which*.

> The new procedures that were discussed at our last meeting are going into effect as of November 15.
>
> > Notice how the clause *that were discussed at our last meeting* separates the subject *procedures* from the verb *are*.
>
> The archive files, which no one uses very often, are now in the back of the file room instead of the front.
>
> > Notice how the clause *which no one uses very often* separates the subject *files* from the verb *are*.

In place of the word *that* to introduce a subordinate clause, it is possible to have just a verb ending in *ed*. Because the words *that is/are* or *that was/were* are understood, it is not always necessary to include them in the sentence.

> The vendor selected by the team members is to deliver three advanced sales techniques training sessions this year and six next year.
>
> > The clause *selected by the team members* separates the subject *vendor* and the verb *is*.
>
> The plans discussed at last week's meeting are not definite.
>
> > The clause *discussed at last week's meeting* separates the subject *plans* and the verb *are*.

supposed to

Proofread carefully to make sure you have not omitted the final *d* in the word *supposed*.

> He said we are supposed to arrange the files alphabetically.
>> That sentence is correct.
>
> He said we are suppose to arrange the files alphabetically.
>> That sentence is not correct. People who make this mistake do not hear the *d* in spoken English. The *t* in *to* blends with the *d* in *supposed*.

than/then

Use *than* for comparison.

> For most people, writing on a personal computer is easier than writing on paper.
>
> As we discussed, Widget XL is stronger than Widget SL.
>
> The conference room on the fifth floor is larger than the one on the sixth floor.
>
> Although she is more experienced than any other person in the department, she did not get the promotion.

Associate *then* with *when* to remember that *then* refers to time.

> The team members established their objectives first. Then, they scheduled another meeting to determine an action plan.
>
> I will be on vacation from March 1 to March 10. If I don't hear from you before then, I'll call you when I return.
>
> We will be finishing our market research in September. Then, we will decide on our new direction.

that/which

If you get confused with *that* and *which*, you may remember only some of the rules applying to each word, or you may misunderstand the terminology associated with the rules.

That clauses are referred to as restrictive clauses, essential clauses, defining clauses, adjective clauses and noun clauses. *Which* clauses are referred to as nonrestrictive clauses, nonessential clauses, descriptive clauses and adjective clauses. No wonder people get confused!

You can save yourself some extra thinking time by adhering to the advice in this chapter. Use *that* and *which* for different reasons; do not use them interchangeably.

That

The word *that*: (1) refers to people or things, (2) limits the noun it follows, and (3) never requires commas.

When you use *that* to introduce a group of words, you are usually pinpointing or restricting the word before *that*. Your reader needs this restrictive clause to accurately understand the meaning of the sentence.

> **The records that were reviewed did not indicate a problem.**
>
> > The records referred to are only the ones reviewed. The clause *that were reviewed* limits the word *records* to specific information. Without this clause, the sentence would not have the same meaning.

To remember how *that* clauses are used, associate the word *that* with another use it has: pointing.

> **That is the elevator to take to the 11th floor.**
>
> > Can you picture someone pointing while saying that sentence? The writer or speaker wants you to see only one elevator.
>
> **The résumé that captured my attention had lots of white space and several headings.**
>
> > Note how the words *that captured my attention* point to one specific résumé.

Although *who* and *whom* are generally preferred to the word *that* in references to people, it is also correct to use *that*. The group of words it introduces must limit the word it follows, however.

that/which

> The candidate that scored the most points was less experienced than most of the others.

> The word *that* introduces information limiting the candidate to one specific person. The sentence would also be correct with *who*: The candidate who scored the most points was less experienced than most of the others.

Which

The word *which*: (1) refers to things, not people, (2) introduces additional information as a parenthetical thought, and (3) requires commas in most cases.

Always use *which* — never *that* — to introduce extra information. By using a comma before *which* and after the group of words providing the extra description, you indicate a parenthetical thought.

> The company, which has a fiscal year starting July 1, must complete its budget before it can provide accurate figures for next year.

> You can eliminate the clause *which has a fiscal year starting July 1* without altering the primary meaning of the sentence. The clause adds to the reader's understanding, but it does not limit or pinpoint the word *company* in any way.

Tests to Determine That or Which

The group of words you create with either *that* or *which* is called a clause. Ask yourself two questions about the clause to help you choose *that* or *which*.

- If I take the clause out, does it change the meaning?
- Does the clause answer "Which one?" or "Which ones?"

If you answer "Yes," the word you want is *that*. If you answer "No," the word you want is *which*.

> Business areas that specialize in systems analysis and design are usually referred to as Information Technology.

> If you take out the clause *that specialize in systems analysis and design*, does it change the meaning of the sentence? Yes. It is not true that business areas are usually referred to as Information Technology. Only the ones that specialize in systems analysis and design are referred to as Information Technology.

> Does the clause answer the question "Which one?" or "Which ones?" Yes. Which business areas? The ones that specialize in systems analysis and design.

Business Style Guide

that/which

Cutting *That*

Sometimes you can be more concise by cutting the word *that*. Just be careful not to eliminate words your reader needs.

> The summary that I faxed to you this morning does not include travel costs.
>> Eliminating *that* does not cause a problem for your readers: The summary I faxed to you this morning does not include travel costs.
>
> When you meet with David tomorrow, be sure to ask about anything that could affect our billing procedures.
>> If you eliminated the word *that*, the sentence would not make sense.

Which *Hunting*

If you are presenting technical information to a nontechnical audience, watch out for the word *which*. In your effort to explain details, you may try to pack too much information into one sentence. Frequently, you can lift out *which* clauses and make them separate sentences. "*Which* hunting" can help you create a more readable document.

> On March 13, the storage utilization on the H078 jumped from an average of 600K to over 3000K due to job S38714D, which ran from 9:30 A.M. until 10:40 A.M.
>
> On March 13, the storage utilization on the H078 jumped from an average of 600K to over 3000K due to job S38714D. This job ran from 9:30 A.M. until 10:40 A.M.
>> Instead of the word *which* introducing extra information in one sentence, the word *This* starts a new sentence referring to information in the first one.

the reason being

Although you may hear people use this expression in conversation, do not use it in writing. The word *being* cannot function by itself as a verb in a sentence.

> The records are being reviewed by the audit team this week.
>> The verb in that sentence is *are being reviewed*. Note that the word *being* is one of three words making up the verb.
>
> We are not going to consider any other alternatives. The reason being that we don't have time.
>> The second sentence is not correct. You can correct it by using a different verb — *is* — that functions by itself: **The reason is that we don't have time.**

Another choice is to rephrase a sentence completely rather than use *the reason being*.

> Since we do not have time, we are not going to consider any other alternatives.
>
> We are not going to consider any other alternatives because we do not have time.

Refer to page 36 for an explanation of a similar phrase: *the reason is because*. Also check page 37 for advice about the expression *being that*.

Business Style Guide

used to

Proofread carefully to make sure you have not omitted the final *d* in the word *used*.

> We used to press the Enter key to begin the processing of these reports.
>> That sentence is correct.

> We use to press the Enter key to begin the processing of these reports.
>> That sentence is not correct. People who make this mistake do not hear the *d* in spoken English. The *t* in *to* blends with the *d* in *used*.

---

who/whom

In most business documents, *who* is necessary more often than *whom*. Because the complete understanding of these words requires considerable skill in analyzing sentence structure, you may be better off rearranging the sentence than taking time to analyze the grammar!

Who always functions as the subject, and it always comes before a verb.

> Ms. Dietrich is the customer who called about an incorrect invoice.
>> Note that the verb *called* occurs immediately after the word *who*.

Whom always functions as the *object*, and it always comes after words such as *to* and *for*.

> To whom did you send the revised letter?

In both of the examples on this page, it is possible to rearrange the sentences to avoid using either *who* or *whom*.

> Ms. Dietrich called about an incorrect invoice.

> Which customers received the revised letter?

whose/who's

People confuse these two words because the way to form the possessive of most words is to add an apostrophe and *s*.

> Bob's briefcase
>
> Heather's suggestion

However, pronouns such as *whose* do not follow that rule. *Whose* shows possession but it does not require an apostrophe.

> The person whose plan is most cost effective will be the person selected.

Typical business usage requires *who's* more often than *whose* because you are often writing about who is doing something. *Who's* is the contraction for *who is*.

> Cameron is the manager who's coordinating the project.

Business Style Guide

you/your with *ing* Words

A typical way to ask someone to do something in business is to use the words *I would appreciate* and then give a direction. If you choose to use this phrasing, you may become stumped when you use a gerund (a word ending in *ing*) as part of your direction.

> I would appreciate your sending me the videotape of his training session.
>
> > Does the word *your* sound correct to you? It is.

Here's why you need *your*, not *you*, before an *ing* word such as *sending*: The word *sending* is a gerund which functions as a noun; the pronoun *you* cannot describe a noun.

> Your computer is now hooked up to the network.
>
> > The word *computer* is a noun; it requires the possessive pronoun *your*, not *you*, to describe it.

Fortunately, the situations in business that call for the word *your* before a gerund (*ing* word) are limited to typical expressions such as *I would appreciate*. If you're not sure about the sentence, remember that you always have a choice of rephrasing it to something that you know is right.

> I would appreciate your taking some time to review last quarter's reports.
>
> > The word *your* before *taking* is correct. However, you could easily rephrase the sentence if you were not sure: **I would appreciate it if you would take some time to review last quarter's reports.**
>
> I would appreciate your giving this proposal your immediate attention.
>
> > The word *your* before *giving* is correct. However, you could easily rephrase the sentence if you were not sure: **Please give this proposal your immediate attention.**

167

your/you're

Your is possessive. It always describes the word or words immediately following it.

> Your technical knowledge is exactly what we need for this project.
>> The word *your* describes *knowledge*.

> Although we are not pleased with your speed in word processing, your accuracy rate is very high.
>> The first *your* describes *speed*; the second *your* describes *accuracy rate*.

> As soon as you provide the correct form, we will send your reimbursement.
>> *Your* describes *reimbursement*.

You're means "you are." It is a contraction.

> You're the person we want for this technical task.

> You're responsible for completing the project on time.

> When you're reviewing the records, look for opportunities to contact clients who used to do business with us.

Substitution Test

If you consistently make mistakes with *your* and *you're*, try using a substitution test with the words *his* and *he's*. Both *his* and *your* are possessive; both *he's* and *you're* are contractions. You never make mistakes with *his* or *he's* because they sound completely different.

> I will be calling you to check on your plans for the October trade show.
>> Is it logical grammatically to say *his* plans? Yes, and therefore you know that *your* is correct.

> Let me know when you're returning.
>> Is it logical grammatically to say *he's* returning? Yes, and therefore you know that *you're* is correct.

> Your work has shown me that you're making every effort to improve.
>> Here's the test to help you see the difference: His work has shown me that he's making every effort to improve.

your/you're

Why Apostrophes Cause Confusion

Note that the contractions *you're* and *he's* have apostrophes. The purpose of an apostrophe in a contraction is to tell people that one or more letters are missing.

People get confused because nouns that show possession have apostrophes. Several pronouns in English, however, show possession but do not use apostrophes: *your, yours, his, her, hers, their, theirs, its, our, ours, my* and *mine*.

> Wanda's proposal presented three alternatives.
>
>> The word *Wanda's* shows possession. As with most nouns, you form the possessive of *Wanda* by adding an apostrophe and *s*.
>
> Alex's proposal was better organized than hers.
>
>> The word *hers* shows possession, but it does not need an apostrophe.

169

Business Judgement

Simple Steps to E-mail Success

The business world has always had rules—many of them unspoken and not documented—but everyone comes to know what's acceptable and what's not. Be sure to stay on top of expectations, priorities and protocol within your organization. It's so easy to use e-mail, but your computer is not equipped with a Good Judgment key. Business decisions are still up to you.

Always make decisions based on (1) your reader and (2) the content of your message. Considering these two factors will help you choose how much detail to include, when to send copies to others, and when to use special e-mail features. You may even decide to use another means of communicating altogether.

Privacy

Although it's improbable that systems administrators or hackers are looking at your mail, it *is* possible. Remember also, that employers own their e-mail systems; they can legally inspect anyone's mail.

To be safe, think of e-mail messages as conversations you're having in an open area. When you need to discuss sensitive situations or communicate information you don't want others to know about, use the phone or set up a face-to-face meeting.

> Andrea wishes she had met with Denitia instead of sending an e-mail message. Since Andrea accidentally hit the Reply All key, everyone in her department found out about Denitia's unprofessional manner at a recent convention. How embarrassing and awkward for everyone.

Liability

Since e-mail messages can be used in lawsuits, consider the risk before you say something that could work against you or your organization. Keep in mind that even deleted messages can be retrieved.

> Three years ago, Satish in Quality Assurance and Ryan in Marketing had an e-mail conversation about SafetyOpen, a new product being released. Satish told Ryan:

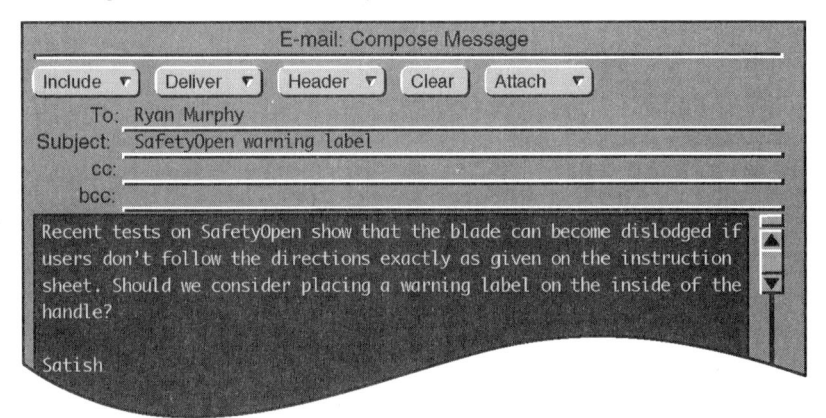

```
E-mail: Compose Message
[Include ▼] [Deliver ▼] [Header ▼] [Clear] [Attach ▼]
      To: Ryan Murphy
 Subject: SafetyOpen warning label
      cc:
     bcc:
Recent tests on SafetyOpen show that the blade can become dislodged if
users don't follow the directions exactly as given on the instruction
sheet. Should we consider placing a warning label on the inside of the
handle?

Satish
```

> Ryan's return message said:

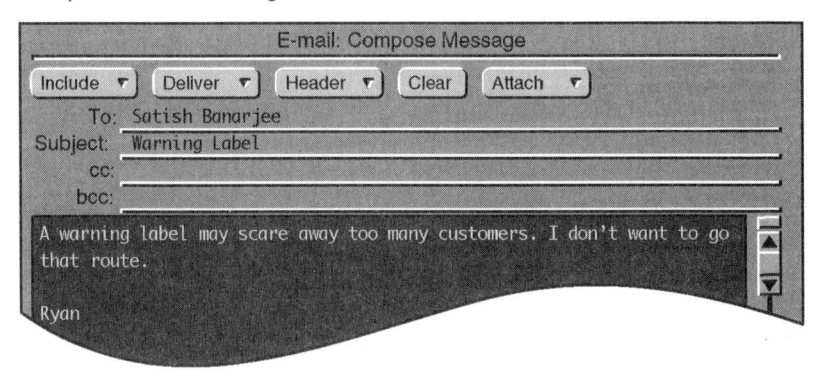

```
E-mail: Compose Message
[Include ▼] [Deliver ▼] [Header ▼] [Clear] [Attach ▼]
      To: Satish Banarjee
 Subject: Warning Label
      cc:
     bcc:
A warning label may scare away too many customers. I don't want to go
that route.

Ryan
```

> Now, as part of a class action suit, lawyers for the plaintiffs have requested electronic retrieval of any message related to SafetyOpen. Would you like to guess who's going to win this one and what the settlement is likely to be?

Business Judgement

E-mail Overload

Before you send copies of your message to a number of people, think about their e-mail load. Are your colleagues receiving hundreds of messages a day? If you gain a reputation for including people who don't need your messages, they may start deleting your messages without even reading them!

> Terry, a programmer analyst in a department of 125 people, sent a message that he would be out of the office for a few days. He had good intentions, but he sent it to everyone. Most of them didn't even know Terry. Would he have made the same decision if his method of communicating had been a memo in the inter-office mail?

If you're concerned about keeping everyone informed and you have a long cc list, add a note at the end of your message to give people a choice:

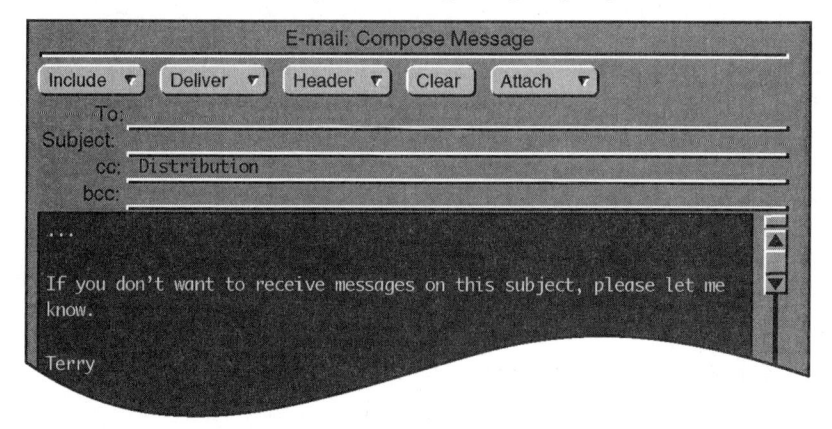

```
                    E-mail: Compose Message
 Include ▼   Deliver ▼   Header ▼   Clear   Attach ▼
        To:
   Subject:
        cc: Distribution
       bcc:
 ...
 If you don't want to receive messages on this subject, please let me
 know.
 Terry
```

173

Response Time

The instant nature of e-mail creates the illusion that as soon as you send a message the receiver reads it. Your expectations for a quick response may be especially high when you tag your message as urgent.

What is considered a reasonable response time in your company's culture? A good rule of thumb is to post at least some response, if not a complete one, within one business day.

When you know someone is expecting a reply but you must delay, you can use a short "what's happening" message such as the following:

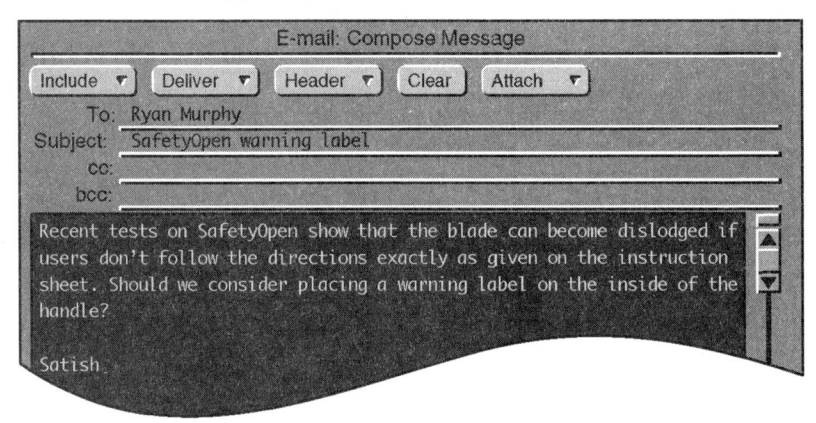

```
                    E-mail: Compose Message
 [ Include ▼ ]  [ Deliver ▼ ]  [ Header ▼ ]  [ Clear ]  [ Attach ▼ ]
       To: Ryan Murphy
  Subject: SafetyOpen warning label
       cc:
      bcc:
 Recent tests on SafetyOpen show that the blade can become dislodged if
 users don't follow the directions exactly as given on the instruction
 sheet. Should we consider placing a warning label on the inside of the
 handle?

 Satish
```

These simple messages don't require a lot of time, and you will enhance your image by responding promptly.

Proactive Communication

Choose some method of managing your mail when you're away. An auto response, for example, will send a reply such as, "I'll be on vacation until November 17," to anyone who sends you a message.

Another option is to ask someone to read your mail and respond for you. You can auto forward your mail to this person or set up a temporary password that this individual can use.

Your proactive communication can keep business operations moving smoothly and save you a few "headaches" when you return.

Business Judgement

Just the Facts

When you communicate in person, people are influenced 55% by your non-verbals, 38% by your tone of voice, and only 7% by the actual words you use. (These statistics are based on a well-known study by Albert Mehrabian, Ph.D., Professor of Psychology at U.C.L.A.)

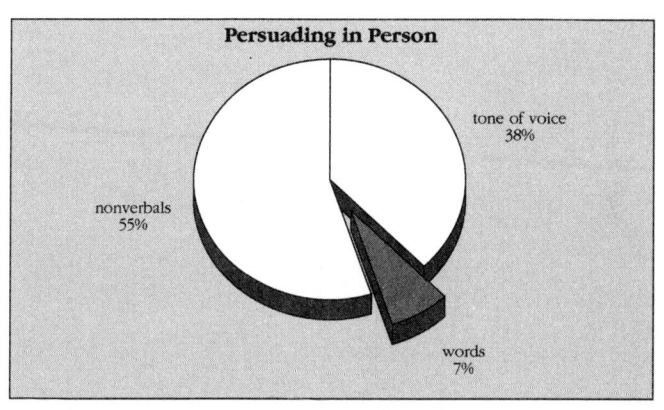

Persuading in Person

- nonverbals 55%
- tone of voice 38%
- words 7%

Accept the fact that humor and irony are extremely difficult to convey in words on a screen. Why take the chance that someone might misinterpret you? Stick to the facts and just the facts.

Using E-Mail Software

Netscape Messenger

Internet Explorer, Outlook Express

America Online E-mail

Netscape Messenger: 1

◆ Configure Netscape Mail ◆ Start Netscape Messenger
◆ The Message List Window ◆ Get New Mail ◆ Read Messages
◆ Delete a Message ◆ Print Messages ◆ Bookmark a Message

Configure Netscape Mail

√ *This section assumes that you have already set up an e-mail account with a service provider. If you do not have an e-mail address, contact your Internet Service Provider. Establishing a modem connection and configuring your computer to send and receive mail can be frustrating. Don't be discouraged; what follows are steps that will get you connected, but some of the information may have to be supplied by your Internet Service Provider. Calling for help will save you time and frustration.*

- The Netscape Communicator browser suite includes a comprehensive e-mail program called Netscape Messenger. Before you can use Messenger to send and receive e-mail, you must configure the program with your e-mail account information (user name, e-mail address, and mail server names). You may have already filled in this information if you completed the New Profile Setup Wizard when you installed Netscape Communicator.

- You may have configured Netscape Messenger to receive and send e-mail messages when you first installed the program. If not, follow these steps to get connected. You can also use these steps to update and change settings to your e-mail account.

Identity Settings

- Open the Edit menu on the Netscape Navigator or Netscape Messenger menu and select Preferences. Click Identity in the Mail & Groups Category list to and do the following:

    Enter your name and e-mail address in the first two boxes. Enter any other optional information in the Identity dialog box.

Netscape Messenger: 1

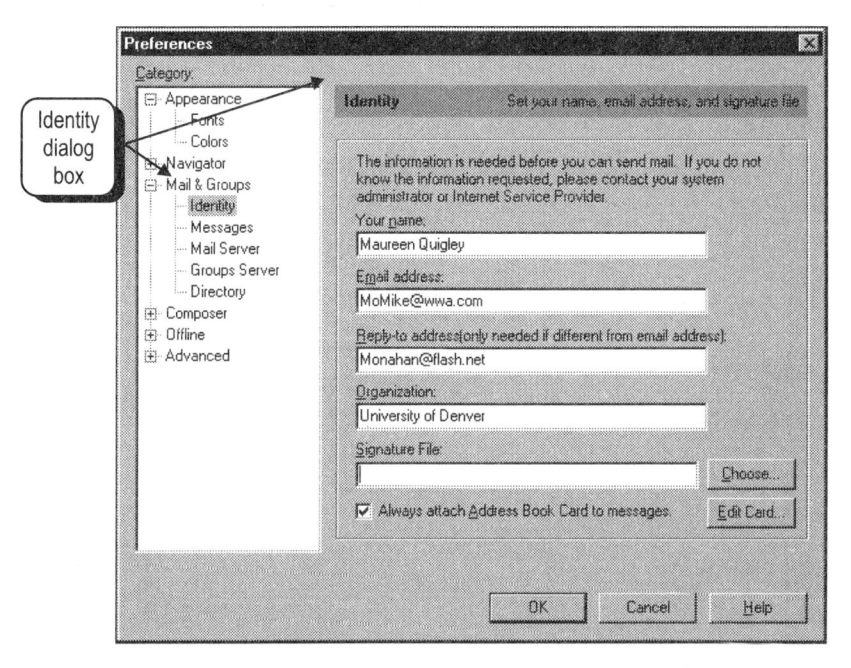

(Identity dialog box — screenshot of Preferences dialog showing Identity category with fields: Your name: Maureen Quigley; Email address: MoMike@wwa.com; Reply-to address: Monahan@flash.net; Organization: University of Denver; Signature File; Always attach Address Book Card to messages checkbox.)

Mail Server Preference Settings

- Click Mail Server to configure your mailbox so that you can send and receive mail.

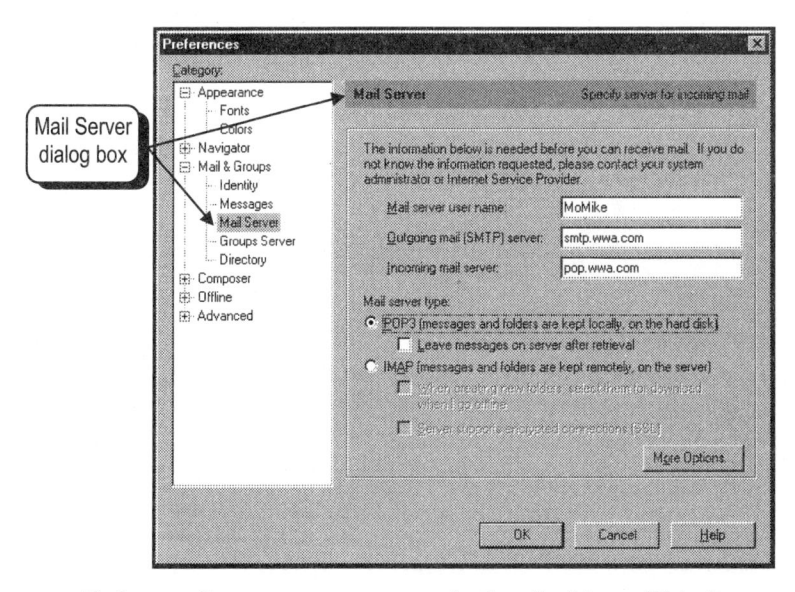

(Mail Server dialog box — screenshot of Preferences dialog showing Mail Server category with fields: Mail server user name: MoMike; Outgoing mail (SMTP) server: smtp.wwa.com; Incoming mail server: pop.wwa.com; Mail server type: POP3 (selected), Leave messages on server after retrieval, IMAP options.)

- Enter mail server user name in the first box. This is usually the part of your e-mail address that appears in front of the @ sign.

Netscape Messenger 179

- Enter your outgoing and incoming mail server. Check with your Internet Service Provider if you are not sure what these settings are.
- Click OK to save and close the Preference settings. You should now be able to send and receive e-mail messages and/or files.

Start Netscape Messenger

- To start Netscape Messenger:
  - Click the Mailbox icon on the Component bar.

The Message List Window

- After you launch Messenger, a message list window will open, displaying the contents of the e-mail Inbox folder.

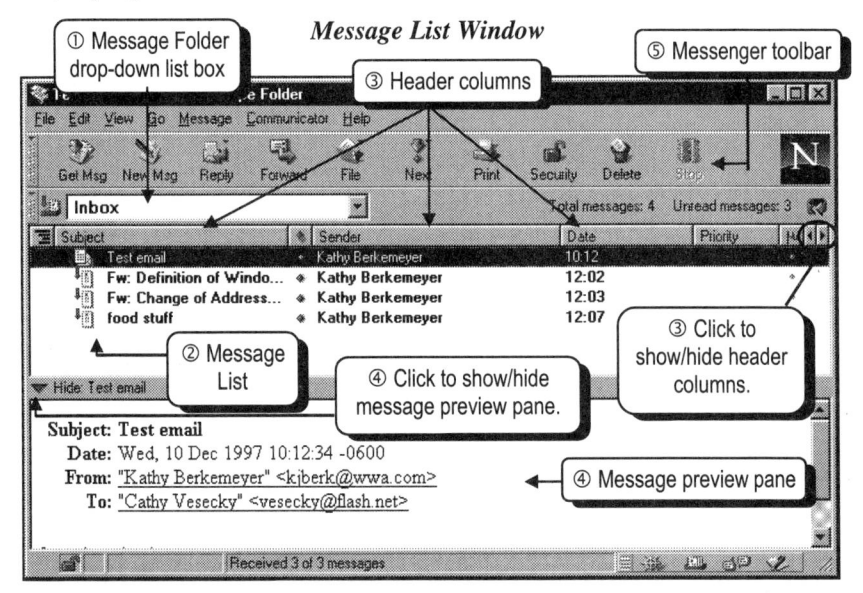

Message List Window

① Message Folder drop-down list box
③ Header columns
⑤ Messenger toolbar
② Message List
④ Click to show/hide message preview pane.
③ Click to show/hide header columns.
④ Message preview pane

- The message list window includes the following:
  - ① The **Message Folder drop-down list box** displays the currently selected message folder, the contents of which are displayed in the message list below the drop-down box. Click the down arrow to display a list of other message folders.
  - ② The **message list** displays a header for each of the messages contained in the currently selected message.
    - **Header columns** list the categories of information available for each message, such as subject, sender, and date.

Netscape Messenger: 1

√ *If text in a message header is cut off so that you cannot read it all, position the mouse pointer on the header in the column containing the cropped text. A small box will display the complete text for that column of the header, as in the example below:*

③ The **message preview pane** displays the content of the message currently selected from the message list. You can show/hide the preview pane by clicking on the blue triangle icon in the bottom-left corner of the message list pane. You can resize the preview pane or the message list pane by placing the pointer over the border between the two panes until the pointer changes to a double arrow and then dragging the border up or down to the desired size.

④ The **Messenger toolbar** displays buttons for activating Netscape Messenger's most commonly used commands.

Messenger Toolbar Buttons and Functions

Button	Function
Get Msg	Retrieves new mail from your Internet mail server and loads it into the Inbox message folder.
New Msg	Opens the Message Composition screen allowing you to compose new mail messages.
Reply	Allows you to reply to the sender of an e-mail message or to the sender and all other recipients of the e-mail message.
Forward	Forwards a message you have received to another address.
File	Stores the current message in one of six Messenger default file folders or in a new folder that you create.
Next	Selects and displays the next of the unread messages in your Inbox.
Print	Prints the displayed message.
Security	Displays the security status of a message.
Delete	Deletes the selected message. Deleted messages are moved to the Trash folder. You must delete contents of Trash folder to remove messages from your computer.

Netscape Messenger   181

Get New Mail

- Since new e-mail messages are stored on a remote ISP mail server, you must be connected to the Internet to access them. To retrieve new messages to your computer, click the Get Msg button ![GetMsg] on the Messenger toolbar.
- In the Password Entry dialog box that follows, enter your e-mail password in the blank text box and click OK. (If you do not know your e-mail password, contact your ISP.)

√ *Messenger saves your password for the rest of the current Messenger session. You must re-enter it each time you retrieve new mail, unless you set Messenger to save your password permanently. To do so:*

  - Click Edit, Preferences.
  - Click once on Mail Server under Mail & Groups.
  - Click the More Options button.
  - Select the Remember my mail password check box and click OK twice.

- The Getting New Messages box opens, displaying the status of your message retrieval.
- Once your new messages are retrieved, they are listed in the message list window. By default, Messenger stores new mail messages in the Inbox folder.

Read Messages

- To open and read a message in a separate window, double-click on the desired message header in the message list. You can close a message after reading it by clicking File, Close or by clicking on the Close button ✕ in the upper-right corner of the window.

- To read the next unread message, click the Next button ![Next] on the Messenger toolbar.

Netscape Messenger: 1

- Once you have read a message, it remains stored in the Inbox folder until you delete it or file it in another folder. (See "Delete a Message" below.)

  √ *You do not have to be online to read e-mail. You can reduce your online charges if you disconnect from your ISP after retrieving your messages and read them offline.*

Delete a Message

- To delete a message, select its header from the message list window and click the Delete button [Delete] in the Messenger toolbar.

  √ *To select more than one message to delete, click the Ctrl button while you click each message header.*

Print Messages

- In order to print a message you must first display the message in either the preview pane of the message list window or in a separate window, then:

  - Click the Print button [Print] on the Messenger toolbar.
  - In the Print dialog box that appears, select the desired print options and click OK.

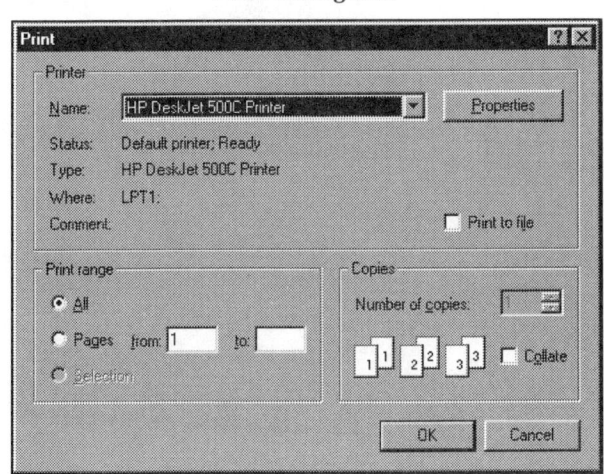

Print Dialog Box

Netscape Messenger 183

Bookmark a Message

- You can add an e-mail message to your Bookmarks folder for easy access from anywhere within the Communicator suite. To bookmark a message:
    - Display the message you want to bookmark in either the preview pane of the message list window or in a separate window.
    - Select Communicator, Bookmarks, Add Bookmark.
- Messenger will add the message to the bottom of your Bookmarks menu.

Netscape Messenger: 2

◆ Compose New Messages ◆ Send Messages
◆ The Message Composition Toolbar ◆ Reply to Mail
◆ Forward Mail ◆ Add Entries to the Personal Address Book
◆ Address a New Message Using the Personal Address Book

Compose New Messages

- You can compose an e-mail message in Netscape Messenger while you are connected to the Internet, or while you are offline. When composing a message offline (which is considered proper Netiquette—net etiquette), you will need to store the message in your Unsent Messages folder until you are online and can send it.

- To create a message, click the New Message button [New Msg].

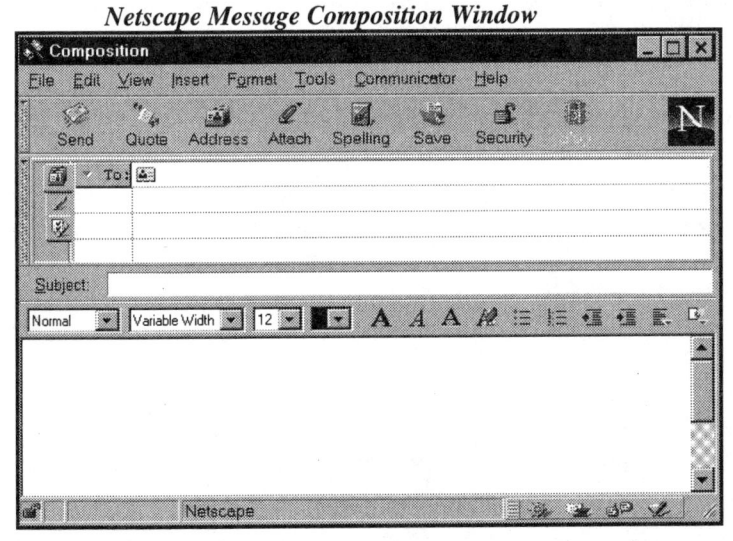

Netscape Message Composition Window

√ If you do not know the recipient's address, you can look it up and insert it from your personal address book (see page 188) or an online directory.

- In the Message Composition window, type the Internet address(es) of the message recipient(s) in the To: field. Or, click the Address button [Address] on the Message Composition toolbar and select an address to insert (see pages 188-190 for more information on using the Address Book).

Netscape Messenger 185

√ *If you are sending the message to multiple recipients, press Enter after typing each recipient's address.*

- After inserting the address(es), click the To: icon to display a drop-down menu of other addressee options. Select any of the following options.

To	The e-mail address of the person to whom the message is being sent.
CC (Carbon Copy)	The e-mail addresses of people who will receive copies of the message.
BCC (Blind Carbon Copy)	Same as CC, except these names will not appear anywhere in the message, so other recipients will not know that the person(s) listed in the BCC field received a copy.
Group	Names of newsgroups that will receive this message (similar to Mail To).
Reply To	The e-mail address where replies should be sent.
Follow-up To	Another newsgroup heading; used to identify newsgroups to which comments should be posted (similar to Reply To).

- Click in the <u>S</u>ubject field (or press Tab to move the cursor there) and type the subject of the message.
- Click in the blank composition area below the Subject field and type the body of your message. You can also check the spelling of your message by clicking on the Spelling button on the Message Composition toolbar and responding to the dialog prompts that follow.

Send Messages

- Once you have created a message, you have three choices:
    - to send the message immediately
    - to store the message in the Unsent Messages folder to be sent later (<u>F</u>ile, Send <u>L</u>ater)
    - to save the message in the Drafts folder to be finished and sent later (<u>F</u>ile, <u>S</u>ave Draft)

    To send a message immediately:

    - Click the Send button on the Message Composition toolbar.

Netscape Messenger: 2

The Message Composition Toolbar

- The toolbar in the Message Composition window has several features that are specific only to this screen.

Message Composition Toolbar

Spelling	Checks for spelling errors in the current message.
Save	Lets you save your message as a draft for later use.
Security	Sets the security status of a message.
Stop	Stops the display of an HTML message or a message with an HTML attachment.

- The Formatting toolbar provides commands for applying styles, fonts, font size, bulleted lists, and inserting objects.
- The remaining toolbar buttons are discussed later in the book's Netscape Messenger section.

Reply to Mail

- To reply to a message, select or open the message to reply to and click the Reply button [Reply].
- From the submenu that appears, select Reply to Sender to reply to the original sender only, or select Reply to Sender and All Recipients to send a reply to the sender and all other recipients of the original message.

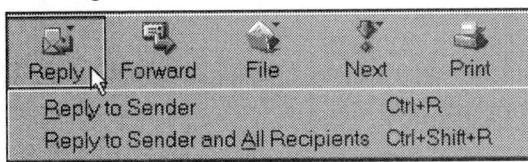

√ *The Message Composition window opens, with the To, Cc, and Subject fields filled in for you.*

- Compose your reply as you would a new message.

- To include a copy of the original message with your reply, click the Quote button [Quote] on the Message Composition toolbar. You can edit the original message and header text as you wish.

- When you are finished, click the Send button [Send] to send the message immediately.

Forward Mail

- To forward a message automatically without having to enter the recipient's name or e-mail address, first select or open the message to forward. Then click on the Forward button [Forward].

  The Message Composition window opens, with the Subject field filled in for you.

  | Subject: | [Fwd: Andy's Birthday Party] |

- Type the e-mail address of the new recipient in the To field, or click the Address button [Address] on the Message Composition toolbar and select a name from your Address Book (see "Address a New Message Using the Personal Address Book" on page 190).

- If the original message does not appear in the composition area, click the Quote button [Quote] on the Message Composition toolbar to insert it.

- Click in the composition area and edit the message as desired.

- When you are done, click the Send button [Send] to send the message immediately. Or, select Send Later from the File menu to store the message in the Unsent Messages mailbox to be sent later. To save the reply as a draft to be edited and sent later, select Save Draft from the File menu.

Add Entries to the Personal Address Book

- You can compile a personal address book to store e-mail addresses and other information about your most common e-mail recipients. You can then use the address book to find and automatically insert an address when creating a new message.

Netscape Messenger: 2

- To add a name to the address book:
  - Select <u>A</u>ddress Book from the <u>C</u>ommunicator menu. The Address Book window displays.

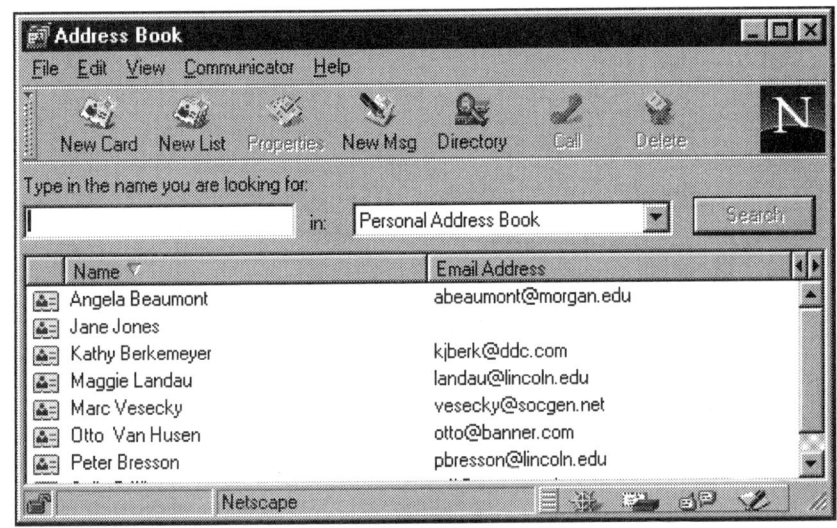

  - Click the New Card button [New Card] on the Address Book toolbar.
  - In the New Card box that appears, enter the recipient's first name, last name, organization, title, and e-mail address.

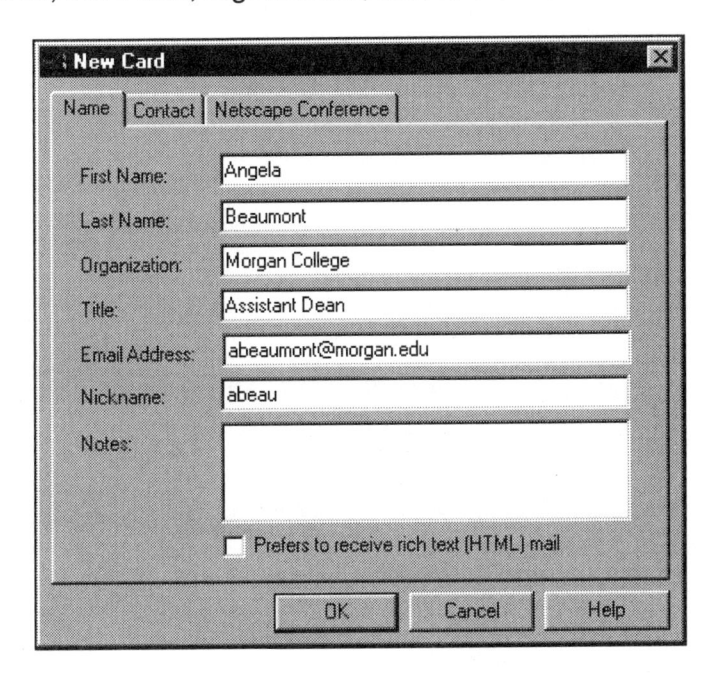

Netscape Messenger 189

- In the Nickname field, type a nickname for the recipient, if desired (the nickname must be unique among the entries in your address book). When addressing a message, you can use the recipient's nickname in the To field, rather than typing the entire address, and Messenger will automatically fill in the full e-mail address.
- In the Notes field, type any notes you want to store about the recipient.
- Click the Contact tab, if desired, and enter the recipient's postal address and phone number.
- Click OK.

■ You can edit an address book entry at any time by double-clicking on the person's name in the Address Book window.

■ You can automatically add the name and address of the sender of a message you are reading by selecting Add to Address Book from the Message menu and selecting Sender from the submenu.

Address a New Message Using the Personal Address Book

■ To insert an address from your address book into a new message:

- Click the New Msg button [New Msg] to open the Message Composition window.

- Click on the Address button [Address] on the Message Composition toolbar and select a recipient(s) from the list in the Address Book window. Drag the selected name(s) into the To field in the Message Composition window. Click the Close button [X] in the Address Book window when you are finished.

OR

- Begin typing the name or nickname of the recipient in the To field of the Message Composition window. If the name is included in the Address Book, Messenger will recognize it and finish entering the name and address for you.

Netscape Messenger: 3

◆ Attached Files ◆ View File Attachments
◆ Save Attached Files ◆ Attach Files to Messages

Attached Files

- Sometimes an e-mail message will come with a separate file(s) attached. Messages containing attachments are indicated when you display a message and it contains a paperclip icon to the right of the message header.

- With Messenger, you can view both plain text attachments and binary attachments. **Binary** files are files containing more than plain text (i.e., images, sound clips, and formatted text, such as spreadsheets and word processor documents).

View File Attachments

- File or HTML attachments are displayed in one of two ways.
    - If you select View, Attachments, Inline, you see the attachment appended to the body of the message in a separate attachment window below the message.

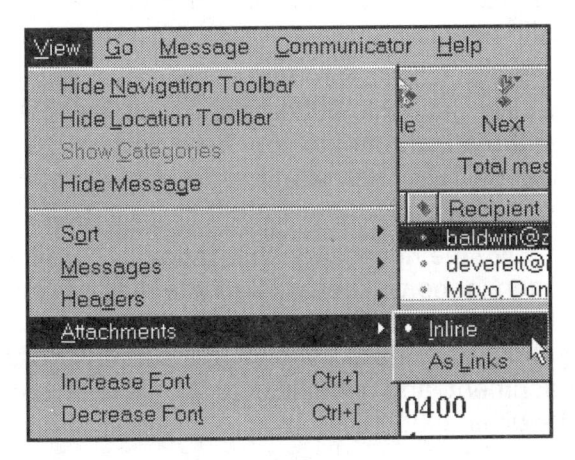

    √ *Only plain text, images, and Web page attachments can be viewed inline.*

    - If you select View, Attachments, As Links, the attachment window displays an attachment box displaying the details of the attachment. It also serves as a link to the attachment.

√ *Viewing attachments as links reduces the time it takes to open a message on screen.*

- Clicking on the blue-highlighted text in the attachment box will display the attachment.

> **Name:** marthastewart.txt
> **Type:** Plain Text (text/plain)
> **Encoding:** 7bit

- You can right-click on the attachment icon box to display a menu of mail options such as forwarding, replying, or deleting the message.

  - By right-clicking on the actual attachment, you can choose from several file save options, such as saving the image or file in a separate file on your hard drive, as Windows wallpaper, or saving the image and putting a shortcut to the image on your desktop.

  - If you open a Web page attachment while online, you will find that the Web page serves as an actual connection to the Web site and that all links on the page are active. If you are not connected, the Web page will display fully formatted, but it will not be active.

- If an attached image displays as a link even after you select View, Attachments, Inline, it is probably because it is an image type that Messenger does not recognize. In this case, you need to install and/or open a plug-in or program with which to view the unrecognized image.

- If you know you have the appropriate application or plug-in installed, click the Save File button in the Unknown File Type dialog box and save the attachment to your hard drive or disk (see "Save Attached Files" below). Then start the necessary application or plug-in and open the saved attachment file to view it.

- If you do not have the necessary application or plug-in, click on the More Info button in the Unknown File Type dialog box. The Netscape Plug-in Finder Web page opens, displaying some general information about plug-ins, a list of plug-ins that will open the selected attachment, and hyperlinks to Web sites where you can download the given plug-ins.

Save Attached Files

- You can save an attached file to your hard drive or disk for future use or reference. To save an attachment:
  - Open the message containing the attachment to save.

Netscape Messenger: 3

- If the attachment is in inline view, convert it to a link (<u>V</u>iew, <u>A</u>ttachments, As <u>L</u>inks).
- Right-click on the link and select <u>S</u>ave Link As.

OR

- Click on the link to open the attachment. Select <u>F</u>ile, Save <u>A</u>s, or, if Messenger does not recognize the attachment's file type, click the <u>S</u>ave File button in the Unknown File Type dialog box.

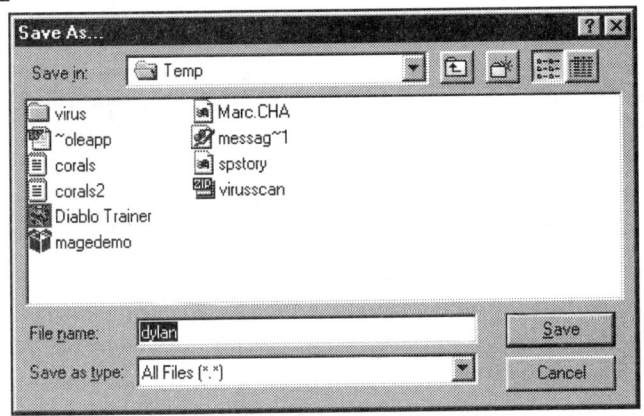

- In the Save As dialog box that follows, click the Save <u>i</u>n drop-down list box and select the drive and folder(s) in which to save the file.
- Click in the File <u>n</u>ame text box and type a name for the file.
- Click <u>S</u>ave.

Attach Files to Messages

- With Messenger, you can attach both plain text and binary files (images, media clips, formatted text documents, etc.) to e-mail messages. You may wish to check if your recipient's e-mail software can decode MIME or UUEncode protocols. Otherwise, binary attachments will not open and display properly on the recipient's computer.
- To attach a file to an e-mail message:

  - Click the Attach button on the Message Composition toolbar, and select <u>F</u>ile from the drop-down menu that appears.
  - In the Enter file to attach dialog box that follows, click the Look <u>i</u>n drop-down list box and select the drive and folder containing the file to attach.

Netscape Messenger 193

- Then select the file to attach and click <u>O</u>pen.

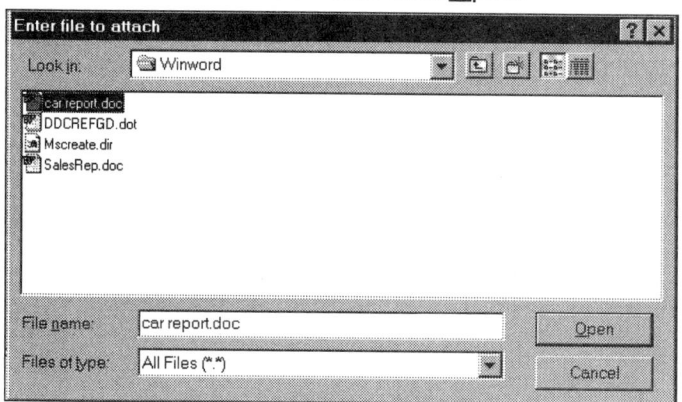

- After you have attached a file, the Attachments field in the Mail Composition window displays the name and location of the attached file.

  √ *Messages containing attachments usually take longer to send than those without attachments. When attaching very large files or multiple files, you may want to zip (compress) the files before attaching them. To do so, both you and the recipient need a file compression program, such as WinZip or PKZip.*

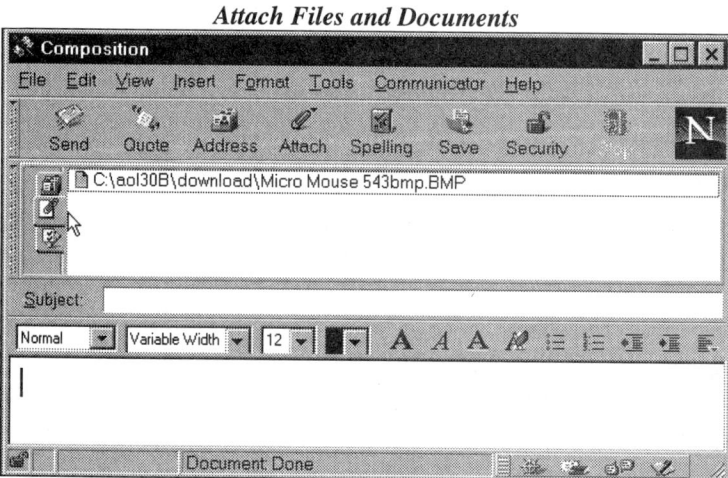

  Attach Files and Documents

- Once you have attached the desired files and finished composing your message, you can send the e-mail, save it in the Unsent Messages folder for later delivery, or save it as a draft for later editing.

Outlook Express: 4

◆ Configure Outlook Express ◆ Start Outlook Express
◆ Outlook Express Main Window ◆ Retrieve New Messages
◆ The Mail Window ◆ Read Messages ◆ Delete a Message
◆ Print a Message ◆ Save a Message

Configure Outlook Express

√ *This section assumes that you have already set up an e-mail account with a service provider. If you do not have an e-mail address, contact your Internet Service Provider. Establishing a modem connection and configuring your computer to send and receive mail can be frustrating. Don't be discouraged. What follows are steps that will get you connected, but some of the information may have to be supplied by your Internet Service Provider. Calling for help will save you time and frustration.*

- Outlook Express is the e-mail program included in the Microsoft Internet Explorer 4.0 suite. With this program, you can send, receive, save, and print e-mail messages and attachments.

- Before you can use Outlook Express to send and receive e-mail, you must configure the program with your e-mail account information (user name, e-mail address, and mail server names).

- You may have already filled in this information if you completed the Internet Connection Wizard when you started Internet Explorer for the first time. If not, you can enter the information by running the Internet Connection Wizard again.

Internet Connection Wizard

- Launch Outlook Express. Open the Tools menu, select Accounts. Click the Mail tab. Click Add and select Mail to start the Connection Wizard.

- The Internet Connection Wizard will ask for information necessary to set up or add an e-mail account.

- Enter the name you want to appear on the "From" line in your outgoing messages. Click Next.

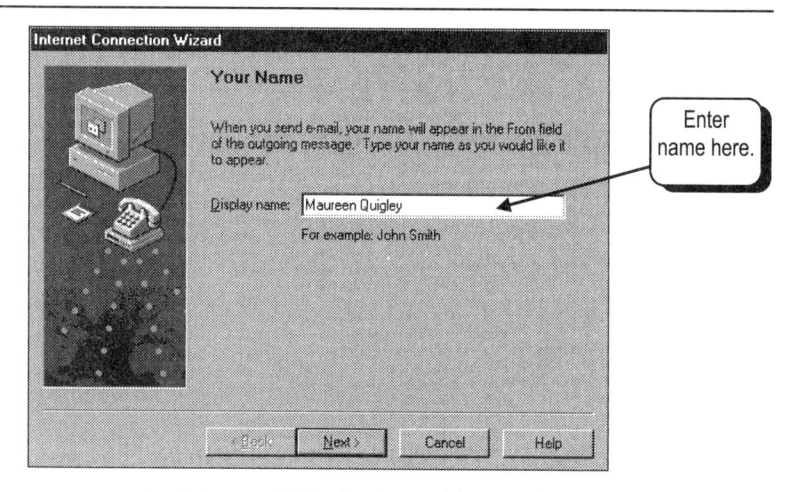

Screenshot of Internet Connection Wizard "Your Name" dialog with Display name "Maureen Quigley". Callout: "Enter name here."

- Type your e-mail address. This is the address that people use to send mail to you. You usually get to create the first part of the address (the portion in front of the @ sign); the rest is assigned by your Internet Service Provider. Click Next.
- Enter the names of your incoming and outgoing mail servers. Check with your Internet Service Provider if you do not know what they are. Click Next.

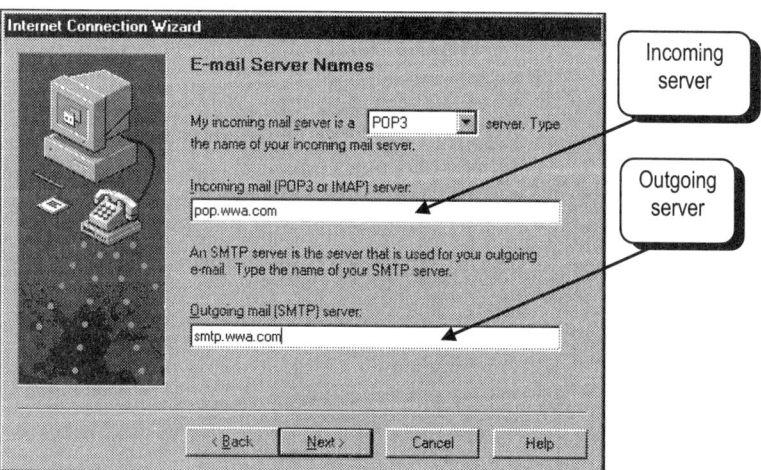

Screenshot of Internet Connection Wizard "E-mail Server Names" dialog with POP3 selected, incoming mail server "pop.wwa.com", and outgoing mail server "smtp.wwa.com". Callouts: "Incoming server" and "Outgoing server."

- Enter the logon name that your Internet Service Provider requires for you to access your mail. You will probably also have to enter a password. The password will appear as asterisks (******) to prevent others from knowing it. Click Next when you are finished.
- Enter the name of the account that will appear when you open the Accounts list on the Tools menu in Outlook Express. It can be any name that you choose. Click Next when you have finished.

Outlook Express: 4

- Select the type of connection that you are using to reach the Internet. If you are connecting through a phone line, you will need to have a dial-up connection. If you have an existing connection, click Next and select from the list of current connections.

- Select an existing dial-up connection, or select Create a new dial-up connection and follow the directions to create a new one.

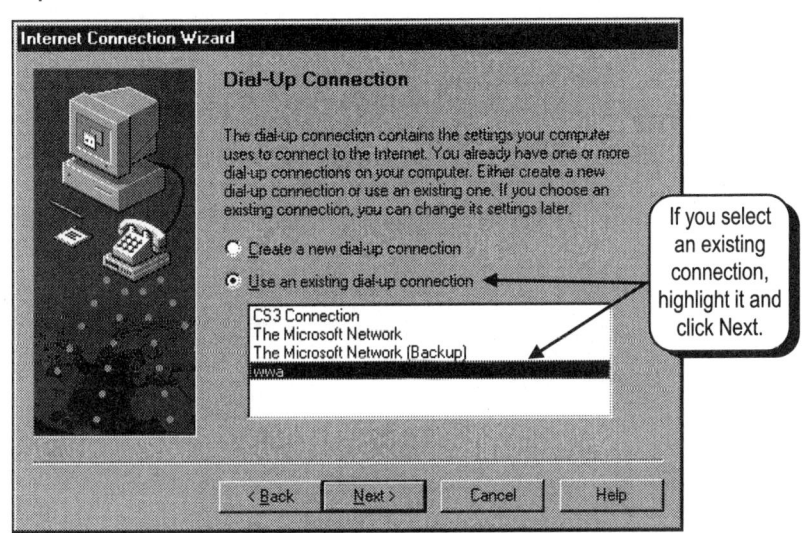

If you select an existing connection, highlight it and click Next.

- If you select Use an existing dial-up connection you will click Finish in the last window to save the settings. You should then be able to launch Outlook Express and send and receive mail and attachments.

Start Outlook Express

■ To start Outlook Express:

- Click the Mail icon on the taskbar.

√ *There is a chance that clicking the Mail icon from the Explorer main window will take you to the Microsoft Outlook organizational program. To use the more compact Outlook Express as your default mail program, click View, Internet Options from the Explorer main window. Click the Programs tab and choose Outlook Express from the Mail pull-down menu.*

√ *If you downloaded Internet Explorer 4, be sure that you downloaded the standard version, which includes Outlook Express in addition to the Web browser.*

Outlook Express Main Window

- After you launch Outlook Express, the main Outlook Express window opens by default. You can access any e-mail function from this window.

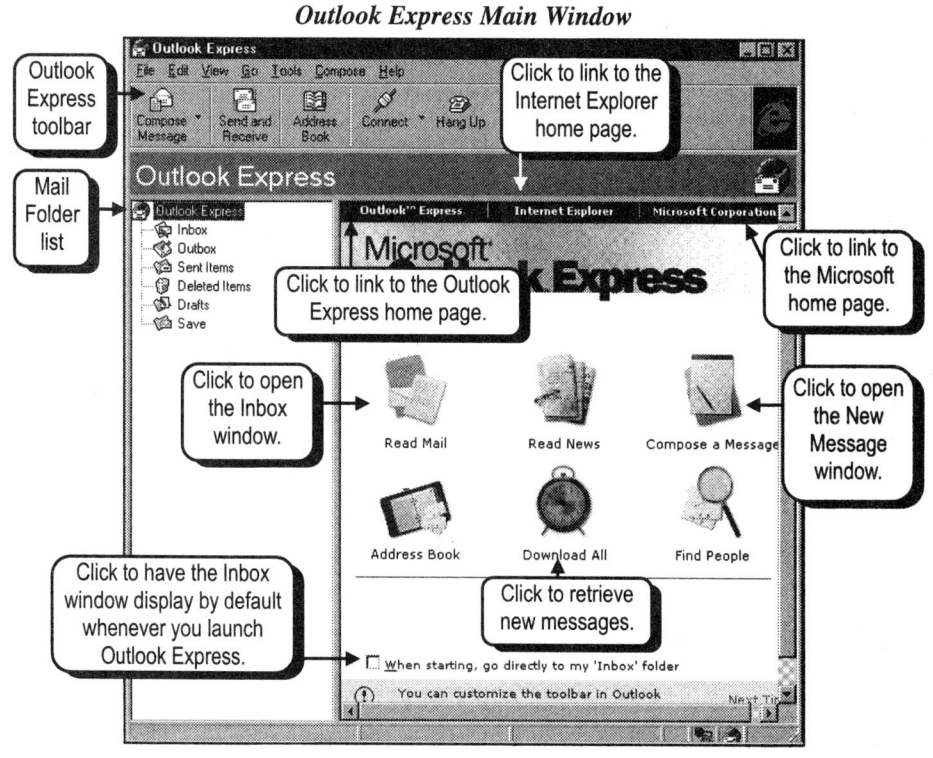

Outlook Express Main Window

[Screenshot of Outlook Express main window with the following callouts:
- Outlook Express toolbar
- Mail Folder list
- Click to link to the Internet Explorer home page.
- Click to link to the Outlook Express home page.
- Click to link to the Microsoft home page.
- Click to open the Inbox window.
- Click to open the New Message window.
- Click to have the Inbox window display by default whenever you launch Outlook Express.
- Click to retrieve new messages.]

- Descriptions of items in the main window follow below:
  - The **Mail Folder list** displays in the left column of the window, with the Outlook Express main folder selected. To view the contents of a different folder, click on the desired folder in the folder list.
  - **Shortcuts** to different e-mail functions are located in the center of the window. Click once on a shortcut to access the indicated task or feature.
  - **Hyperlinks** to Microsoft home pages are located at the top of the window. Click once to connect to the indicated home page.
  - The **Outlook Express toolbar** displays buttons for commonly used commands.

Outlook Express: 4

Retrieve New Messages

- You can access the retrieve new mail command from any Outlook Express window. To do so:

  - Click the Send and Receive button [Send and Receive] on the toolbar.

- In the Connection dialog box that displays, enter your ISP user name in the User Name text box and your password in the Password text box and click OK. (If you do not know your user name or password, contact your ISP.) Outlook Express will send this information to your ISP's mail server in order to make a connection.

  √ *Outlook Express will automatically save your user name and password for the rest of the current Internet session. However, you must re-enter your password each time you reconnect to the Internet or retrieve new mail, unless you set Outlook Express to save your password permanently. To do so, select the **Save Password** check box in the connection dialog box and click OK.*

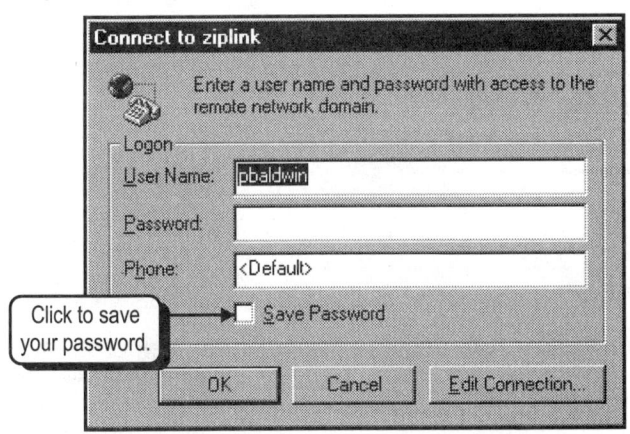

  Connect to ziplink
  Enter a user name and password with access to the remote network domain.
  Logon
  User Name: pbaldwin
  Password:
  Phone: <Default>

  Click to save your password. → ☐ Save Password

  OK   Cancel   Edit Connection...

- Once you are connected to the Internet and Outlook Express is connected to your ISP mail server, new mail messages will begin downloading from your ISP mail server. A dialog box displays the status of the transmittal.

The Mail Window

- After retrieving new messages, Outlook Express stores them in the Inbox folder.

- To view your new messages, you must open the Mail window and display the contents of the Inbox folder. To do so:

Outlook Express 199

- Click the Read Mail shortcut [Read Mail] in the Outlook Express main window.
- The Mail window opens with the Inbox folder displayed. A description of the items in the Mail window appears on the following page:

Mail Window with Inbox Folder Displayed

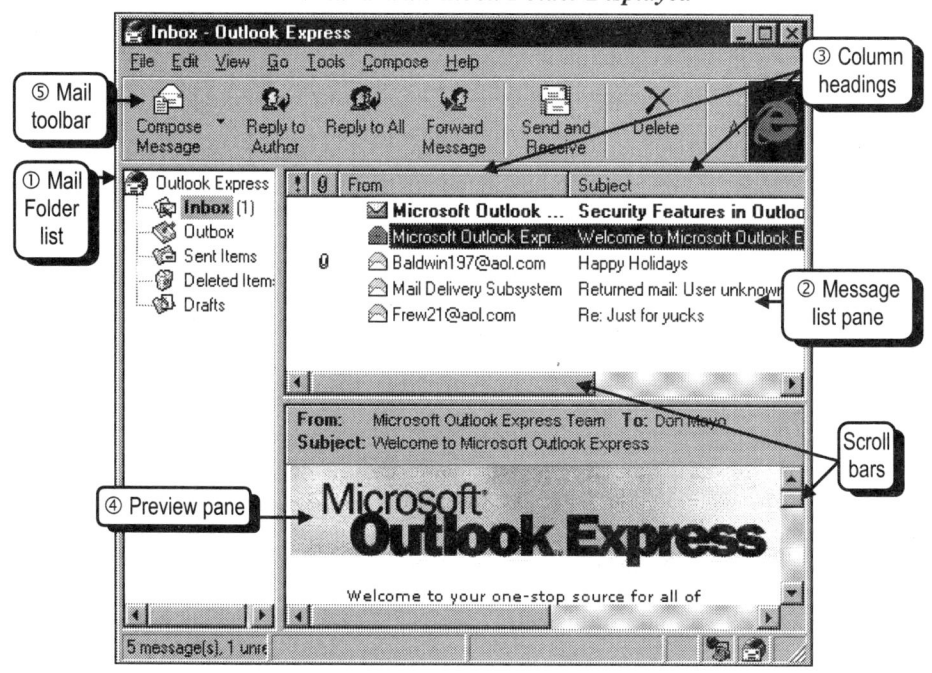

① The **Mail Folder list** displays the currently selected message folder, the contents of which are displayed in the mail list. Click on another folder to display its contents in the mail list.

② The **message list pane** displays a header for each of the messages contained in the currently selected mail folder.

③ **Column headings** list the categories of information included in each message header, such as subject, from, and date received. You can customize the display of the header columns in a number of ways:

- Resize column widths by placing the mouse pointer over the right border of a column heading until the pointer changes to a double arrow and then click and drag the border to the desired size.

- Rearrange the order of the columns by clicking and dragging a column heading to a new location in the series.

④ The **preview pane** displays the content of the message currently selected from the message list. You can show/hide the preview pane by selecting <u>V</u>iew, <u>L</u>ayout and clicking on the Use <u>p</u>review pane check box. You can resize the preview pane or the message list pane by placing the pointer over the border between the two panes until the pointer changes to a double arrow and then dragging the border up or down to the desired size.

⑤ The **Mail toolbar** displays command buttons for working with messages. These commands vary depending on the message folder currently displayed (Inbox, Sent, Outbox, etc.).

Read Messages

√ *You do not have to be online to read e-mail. You can reduce your online charges if you disconnect from your ISP after retrieving your messages and read them offline.*

- You must have the Mail window open and the mail folder containing the message to read displayed.
- You can read a message in the preview pane of the Mail window, or in a separate window.
- To read a message in the preview pane, click on the desired message header in the message list. If the message does not appear, select <u>V</u>iew, <u>L</u>ayout, Use <u>p</u>review pane.
- To open and read a message in a separate window, double-click on the desired message header in the message list.

Message Window

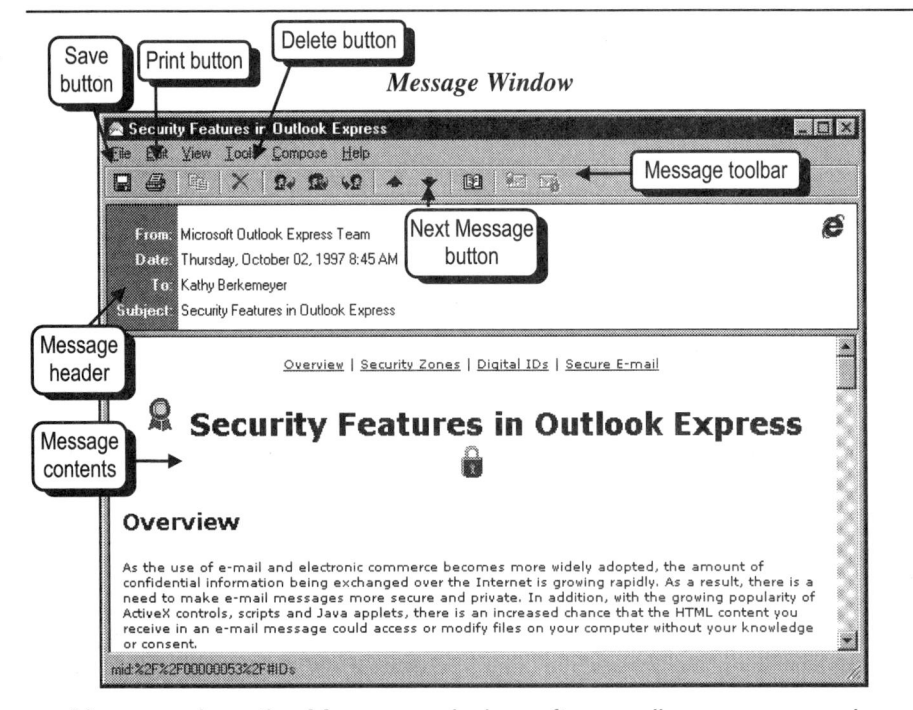

[Screenshot of Outlook Express Message window with labels: Save button, Print button, Delete button, Message toolbar, Next Message button, Message header, Message contents]

- You can close the Message window after reading a message by clicking File, Close or by clicking on the Close button (X) in the upper-right corner of the window.
- Use the scroll bars in the Message window or the preview pane to view hidden parts of a displayed message. Or, press the down arrow key to scroll down through the message.
- To read the next unread message:
  - Select View, Next, Next Unread Message.

  OR

  - If you are viewing a message in the Message window, click the Next button on the Message toolbar.
- Once you have read a message, it remains stored in the Inbox folder until you delete it or file it in another folder. (See "Delete a Message" on the following page.)

Outlook Express: 4

Delete a Message

- To delete a message:
  - Select the desired header from the message list in the Mail window.
  - Click the Delete button [X Delete] in the Mail toolbar, or select Edit, Delete.

  OR
  - Open the desired message in the Message window.
  - Click the Delete button [X] on the Message toolbar.

  √ *To select more than one message to delete, click the Ctrl button while you click each message header.*

Print a Message

- To print a message:
  - Select the message you want to print from the message list in the Mail window or open the message in the Message window.
  - Select Print from the File menu.
  - In the Print dialog box that opens, select the desired print options and click OK.

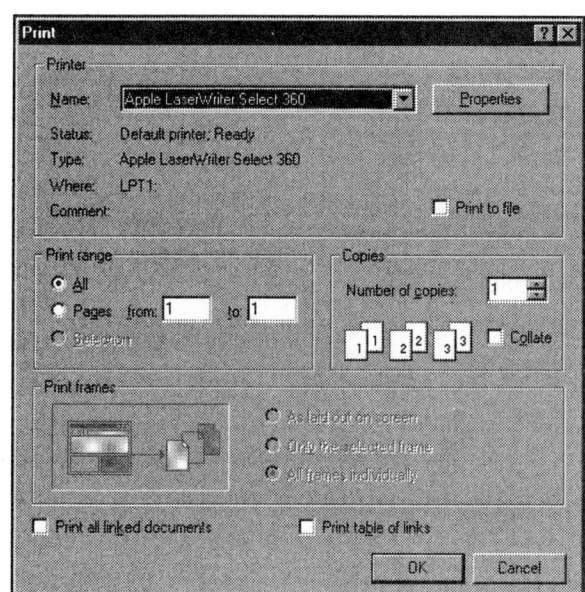

Print Dialog Box

Outlook Express 203

- You can bypass the Print dialog box and send the message to the printer using the most recently used print settings by opening the message in the Message window and clicking the Print button on the Message toolbar.

Save a Message

- To save a message to your hard drive:
    - Open the desired message in the Message window and click the Save button on the Message toolbar.
    - In the Save Message As dialog box that opens, click the Save in drop-down list box and select the drive and folder in which to store the message file.

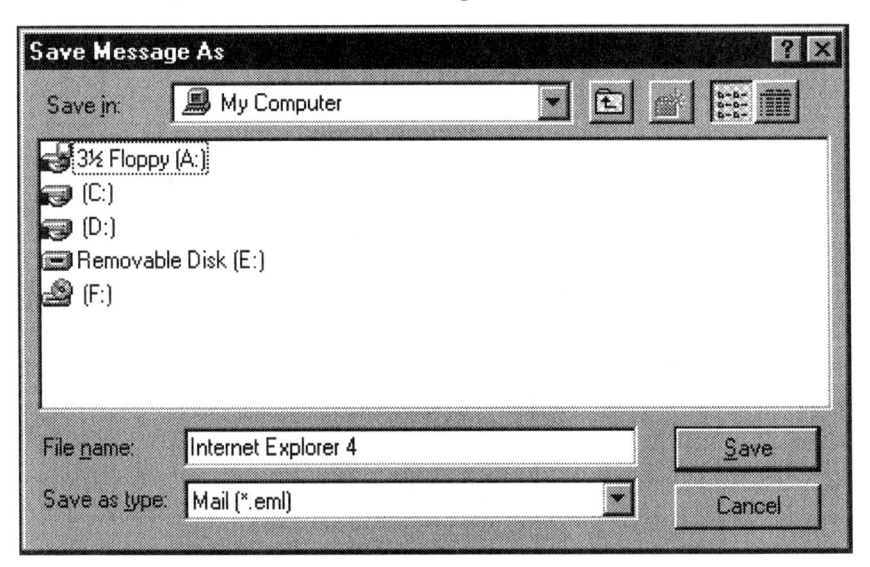

Save Messages As

    - Click in the File name box and enter a name for the message.
    - Click Save.

Outlook Express: 5

◆ Compose New Messages ◆ Send Messages ◆ Reply to Mail
◆ Forward Mail ◆ Add Entries to the Personal Address Book
◆ Address a New Message Using the Personal Address Book

Compose New Messages

- You can compose an e-mail message in Outlook Express while you are connected to the Internet, or while you are offline. When composing a message offline, you will need to store the message in your Outbox folder until you are online and can send it.

- To create a message, you first need to open the New Message window. To do so:

    - Click the New Mail Message button on the toolbar in either the Mail window or the Main window.

    The New Message window displays (see the next page).

    √ *You can hide any toolbar in the New Message window by going to the View menu and deselecting Toolbar, Formatting Toolbar, or Status Bar.*

    - In the New Message window, type the Internet address(es) of the message recipient(s) in the To field.

        √ *If you type the first few characters of a name or e-mail address that is saved in your address book, Outlook Express will automatically complete it for you. (See page xx for information on using the Address Book.)*

    OR

    Click the Index Card icon in the To field or the Address Book button on the New Message toolbar and select an address to insert (see page 211 for information on using the Address Book).

    √ *If you are sending the message to multiple recipients, insert a comma or semicolon between each recipient's address.*

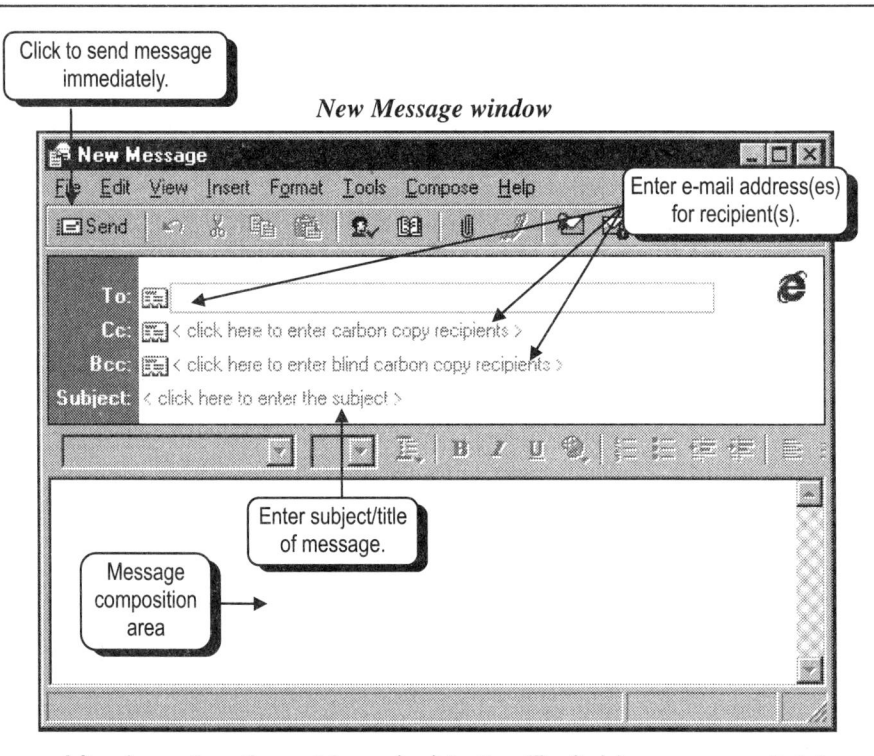

New Message window

- Click to send message immediately.
- Enter e-mail address(es) for recipient(s).
- Enter subject/title of message.
- Message composition area

- After inserting the address(es) in the To field, you may click in either of the following fields and enter the recipient information indicated.

  CC (Carbon Copy)   The e-mail addresses of people who will receive copies of the message.

  BCC (Blind Carbon Copy)   Same as CC, except these names will not appear anywhere in the message, so other recipients will not know that the person(s) listed in the BCC field received a copy.

- Click in the Subject field and type the subject of the message. An entry in this field is required.

- Click in the blank composition area below the Subject field and type the body of your message. You can also check the spelling of your message by selecting Spelling from the Tools menu and responding to the prompts that follow.

Send Messages

- Once you have created a message, you have three choices:
  - to send the message immediately
  - to store the message in the Outbox folder to be sent later

Outlook Express: 5

- to save the message in the Drafts folder to be edited and sent later

To send a message immediately:

√ *To be able to send messages immediately, you must first select Options from the Tools menu in the Mail window. Then click on the Send tab and select the Send messages immediately check box. If this option is not selected, clicking the Send button will not send a message immediately, but will send the message to your Outbox until you perform the Send and Receive task.*

- Click the send button [Send] on the New Message toolbar.

OR

Click File, Send Message.

- Outlook Express then connects to your ISP's mail server and sends out the new message. If the connection to the mail server is successful, the sending mail icon displays in the lower-right corner of the status bar until the transmittal is complete:

[Status bar] → Sending mail...   ← [Sending mail icon]

- Sometimes, however, Outlook Express cannot immediately connect to the mail server and instead has to store the new message in the Outbox for later delivery. When this happens, the sending mail icon does not appear, and the number next to your Outbox folder increases by one [Outbox (1)].

- Outlook Express does not automatically reattempt to send a message after a failed connection. Instead, you need to manually send the message from the Outbox (see "To send messages from your Outbox folder" on page 207).

To store a message in your Outbox folder for later delivery:

- Select File, Send Later in the New Message window.
- The Send Mail prompt displays, telling you that the message will be stored in our Outbox folder.
- Click OK.
- The message is saved in the Outbox.

To send messages from your Outbox folder:

- Click on the Send and Receive button [Send and Receive] on the toolbar.

Outlook Express 207

OR
- Click <u>T</u>ools, <u>S</u>end and Receive, All Accounts.

√ *When you use the Send and Receive command, Outlook Express sends out **all** messages stored in the Outbox and automatically downloads any new mail messages from the mail server.*

- After you click Send and Receive, a dialog box opens, displaying the status of the transmittal.

To save a message to your Drafts folder:
- Click <u>F</u>ile, <u>S</u>ave.
- The Saved Message prompt displays. Click OK.

To edit and send message drafts:
- In the Mail window, click in the Drafts folder [Drafts (1)] from the Mail Folder list.
- Double-click on the desired message header from the message list.
- In the New Message window that appears, edit your message as necessary. When you are finished, select <u>F</u>ile, S<u>e</u>nd Message to send the message immediately, or <u>F</u>ile, Send <u>L</u>ater to store it in the Outbox folder for later delivery.

■ Outlook Express automatically saves all sent messages in the Sent Items folder. To view a list of the messages you have sent, select the Sent Items folder [Sent Items] from the Mail Folder list. The contents will display in the message list pane.

Reply to Mail
■ In Outlook Express, you can reply to a message automatically, without having to enter the recipient's name or e-mail address.

Outlook Express: 5

- When replying, you have a choice of replying to the author and all recipients of the original message or to the author only.
- To reply to the author and all recipients:
  - Select the message you want to reply to from the message list in the Mail window.
  - Click the Reply to All button [Reply to All] on the Mail toolbar.

  OR
  - Right-click on the selected message and select Reply to All.
- To reply to the author only:
  - Click the Reply to Author button [Reply to Author] on the Mail toolbar.

  OR
  - Right-click on the selected message and select Reply to Author.
- Once you have selected a reply command, the New Message window opens with the address fields and the Subject filled in for you.

  √ *You can access all of the mail send commands by right-clicking on the message in the Message list.*

- The original message is automatically included in the body of your response. To turn off this default insertion, select Options from the Tools menu, click on the Send tab, deselect the Include message in reply check box, and click OK.
- To compose your reply, click in the composition area and type your text as you would in a new message.

- When you are done, click the Send button [Send] on the New Message toolbar to send the message immediately. Or, select Send Later from the File menu to store the message in the Outbox folder for later delivery. To save the reply as a draft to be edited and sent later, select Save from the File menu.

Forward Mail

- To forward a message automatically without having to enter the message subject:
    - Select the message to forward from the message list in the Mail window.
    - Click the Forward Message button [Forward Message] on the Mail toolbar.

    The New Message window opens with the original message displayed and the Subject field filled in for you.

- Fill in the e-mail address information by either typing each address or selecting the recipients from your address book. (See "Address a New Message Using the Personal Address Book" on page 212.)

    √ *If you are forwarding the message to multiple recipients, insert a comma or semicolon between each recipient's address.*

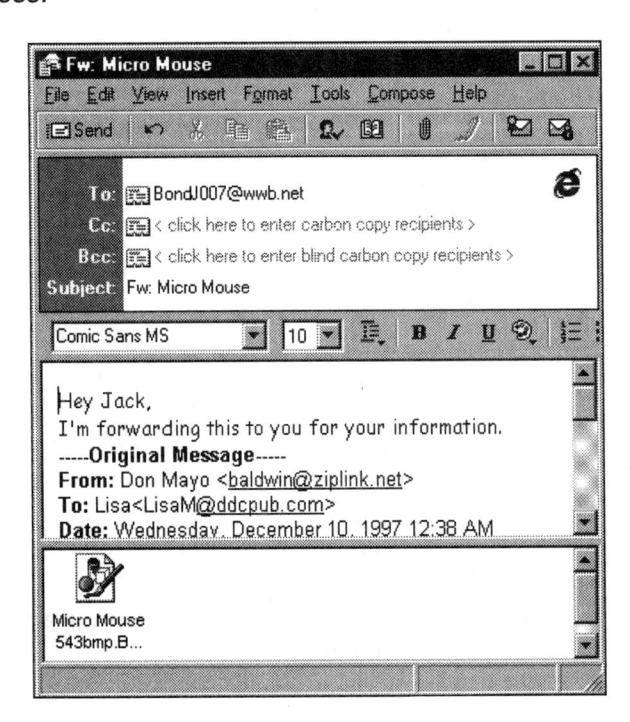

Outlook Express: 5

- Click in the composition area and type any text you wish to send with the forwarded message.

- When you are done, click the Send button ![Send] on the New Message toolbar to send the message immediately. Or, select Send Later from the File menu to store the message in the Outbox folder for later delivery. To save the reply as a draft to be edited and sent later, select Save from the File menu.

Add Entries to the Personal Address Book

- In Outlook Express, you can use the Windows Address Book to store e-mail addresses and other information about your most common e-mail recipients.

- To open the Windows Address Book:

  - Click the Address Book button ![Address Book] on the toolbar in the Mail window or the Main window.

  √ he Address Book window opens, displaying a list of contacts.

  Address Book Window

- To add a name to the address book:

  - Click the New Contact button ![New Contact] on the Address Book toolbar.

  - In the Properties dialog box that displays, type the First, Middle and Last names of the new contact in the appropriate text boxes.

  - Type the contact's e-mail address in the Add new text box and then click the Add button. You can repeat this procedure if you wish to list additional e-mail addresses for the contact.

Outlook Express 211

- In the Nickname text box, you can enter a nickname for the contact (the nickname must be unique among the entries in your address book). When addressing a new message, you can type the nickname in the To field, rather than typing the entire address, and Outlook Express will automatically complete the address.

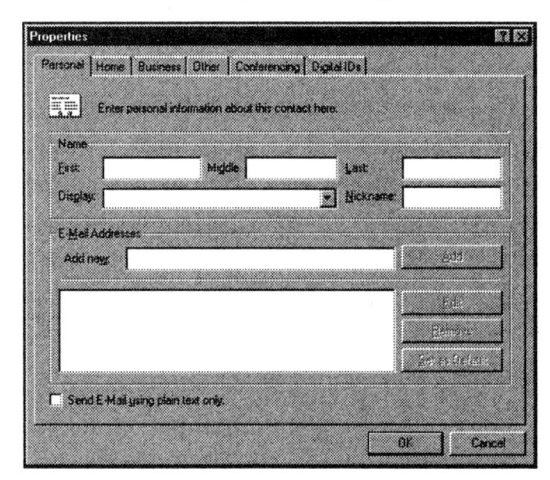

Contact Properties Dialog Box

- You can automatically add the name and address of the sender of a message by opening the message in the Message window, right-clicking on the sender's name in the To field, and selecting Add to Address Book from the shortcut menu.
- You can also set Outlook Express to add the address of recipients automatically when you reply to a message. To do so, select Options from the Tools menu and select the Automatically put people I reply to in my Address Book check box on the General tab.
- You can edit an Address Book entry at any time by double-clicking on the person's name in the contact list in the Address Book window.

Address a New Message Using the Personal Address Book

- To insert an address from your address book into a new message:
  - Click the Select Recipients button 🔲 on the New Message toolbar.
  - In the Select Recipients dialog box that follows, select the address to insert from the contact list.

Outlook Express: 5

Select Recipients Dialog Box

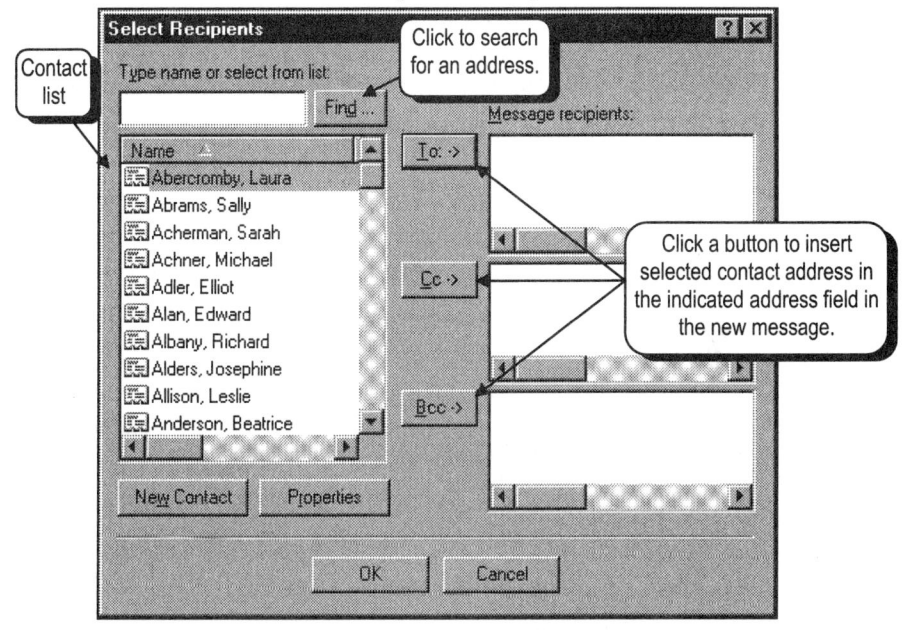

[Figure: Select Recipients dialog box with callouts — "Contact list" pointing to the name list; "Click to search for an address." pointing to the Find button; "Click a button to insert selected contact address in the indicated address field in the new message." pointing to the To, Cc, and Bcc buttons.]

- Click the button for the field in which you want to insert the address (To, Cc, or Bcc). Click OK to return to the New Message window when you are finished.

Outlook Express: 6

◆ **View Attached Files** ◆ **Save Attached Files** ◆ **Attach Files to a Message**

View Attached Files

- Sometimes an e-mail message will come with a separate file(s) attached. Messages containing attachments are indicated in the message list in the Mail window by a paperclip icon 📎 to the left of the message header.

Mail Window

214

Outlook Express: 6

- To view an attachment:
  - Open the folder containing the desired message in the Mail window.
  - Select the message containing the desired attachment(s) from the message list to display it in the preview pane.

  If the attachment is an image, it will display in the message.

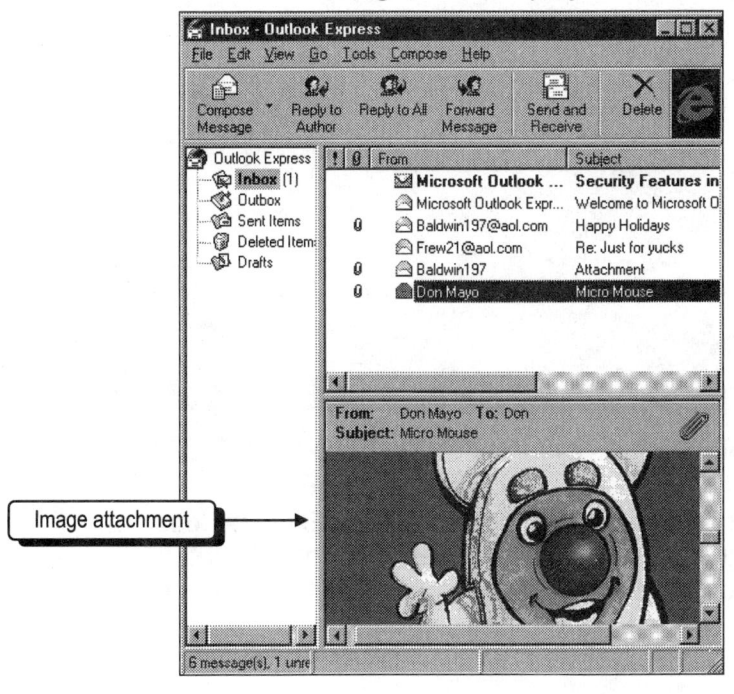

Outlook Express 215

√ *If the image does not display, click Tools, Options, click the Read tab, select the Automatically show picture attachments in messages check box, and click OK.*

- Other types of attachments, such as a program, word processor document, or media clip, do not display in the message, but have to be opened in a separate window. To do so:

    - Click on the attachment icon in the preview pane. A button will display with the file name and size of the attachment.

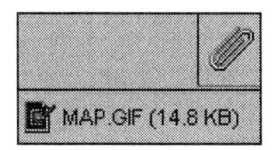

    - Click on this button.
    - If the Open Attachment Warning dialog box displays, select the Open it option and click OK.

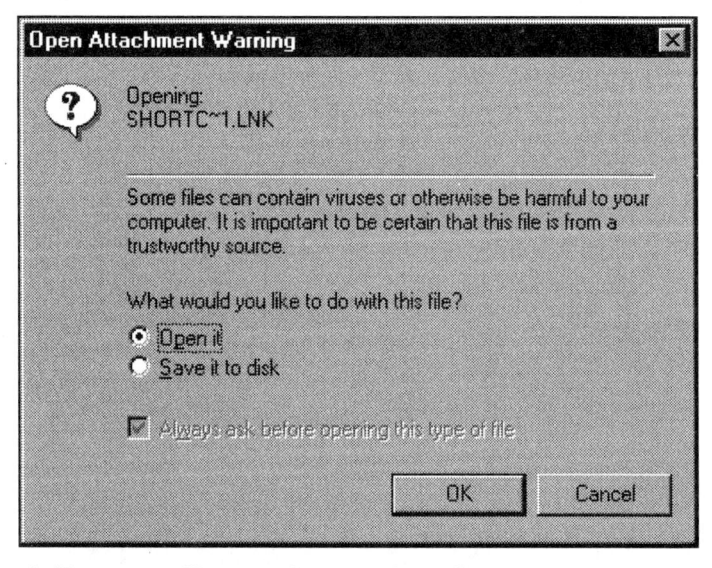

- Outlook Express will open the attached file or play the attached media clip.
- If the attached file does not open, Outlook Express does not recognize the file type of the attached file (that is, Outlook Express does not contain the plug-in, or your computer does not contain the application needed to view it).

Outlook Express: 6

- To view an unrecognized attachment, you have to install and/or open the application or plug-in needed to view it.

Save Attached Files

- If desired, you can save an attached file to your hard drive or disk for future use or reference. To save an attachment:
  - Select Save Attachments from the File menu, and select the attachment to save from the submenu that displays.

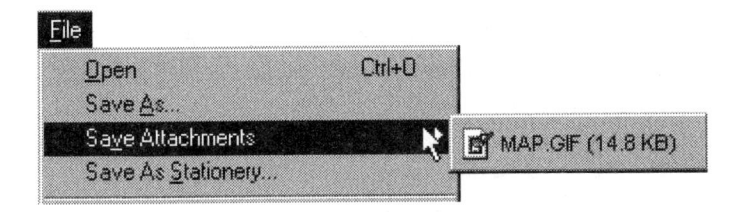

  OR

  - Right-click on the attachment icon in the Message window and select the Save As option.
  - In the Save As dialog box that follows, click the Save in drop-down list box and select the drive and folder in which to save the file.
  - Click in the File name text box and type a name for the file.
  - Click Save.

Attach Files to a Message

- You can attach a file to an e-mail message while composing the message in the New Message window. To add an attachment:
  - Click the Attachments button on the New Message toolbar.

  OR

  - Click Insert, File Attachment.
  - In the Insert Attachment dialog box that appears, click the Look in drop-down list box and select the drive and folder containing the file to attach. Then select the file and click Attach.

Outlook Express 217

Insert Attachment Dialog Box

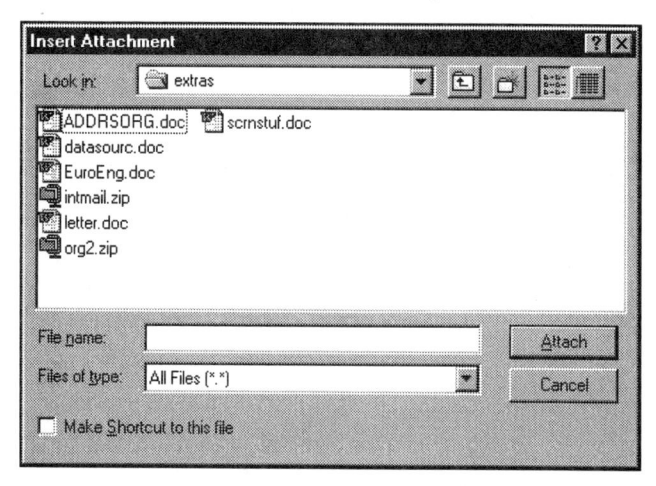

√ *Messages containing attachments usually take longer to send than those without attachments.*

√ *When attaching very large files or multiple files, you may want to zip (compress) the files before attaching them. To do so, both you and the recipient need a file compression program, such as WinZip or PKZip.*

New Message Dialog Box

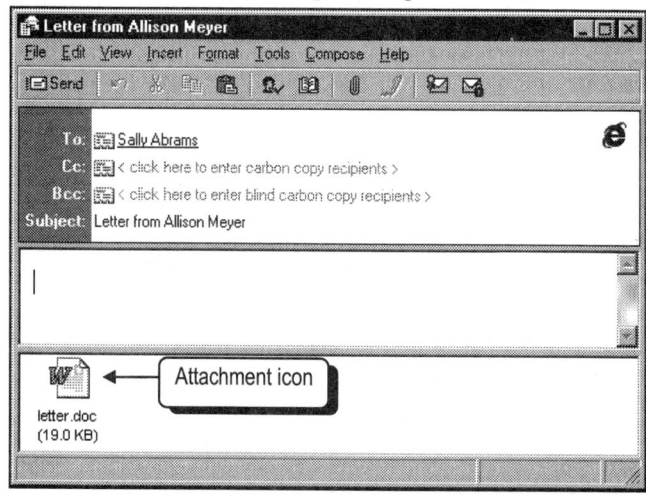

- You can also attach a file by dragging the desired file from your desktop or from Windows Explorer into the New Message window.

  You can add multiple attachments by repeating the procedure.

America Online E-mail: 7

◆ Read New Mail ◆ Compose a New Mail Message ◆ Send Messages
◆ Reply to Mail ◆ Forward Mail ◆ AOL Mail Help

Read New Mail

- There are several ways to know whether you have new mail in your mailbox: If your computer has a sound card and speakers, you will hear "You've Got Mail" when you successfully connect to AOL. The Mail Center link is replaced by the You Have Mail link, and the mailbox icon on the main screen has the flag in the up position You Have Mail.

To display and read new and unread mail:

- Click the You Have Mail button You Have Mail on the AOL main screen.
OR
- Click the Read New Mail button on the main screen toolbar
OR
- Press Ctrl+R.

√ The New Mail list displays new and unread mail for the screen name used for this session. If you have more than one screen name, you must sign on under each name to retrieve new mail.

√ New and Unread e-mail messages remain on the AOL mail server for approximately 27 days before being deleted by AOL. If you want to save a message to your hard disk, click **File, Save As** and choose a location for the message. By default the message will be saved to the Download folder.

- To read a message, double-click on it from the New Mail list.

Compose a New Mail Message

- Click Mail, Compose Mail.
OR
- Click the Compose Mail button on the main screen toolbar.
OR
- Click Ctrl+M.

America Online E-mail 219

The Compose Mail screen displays.

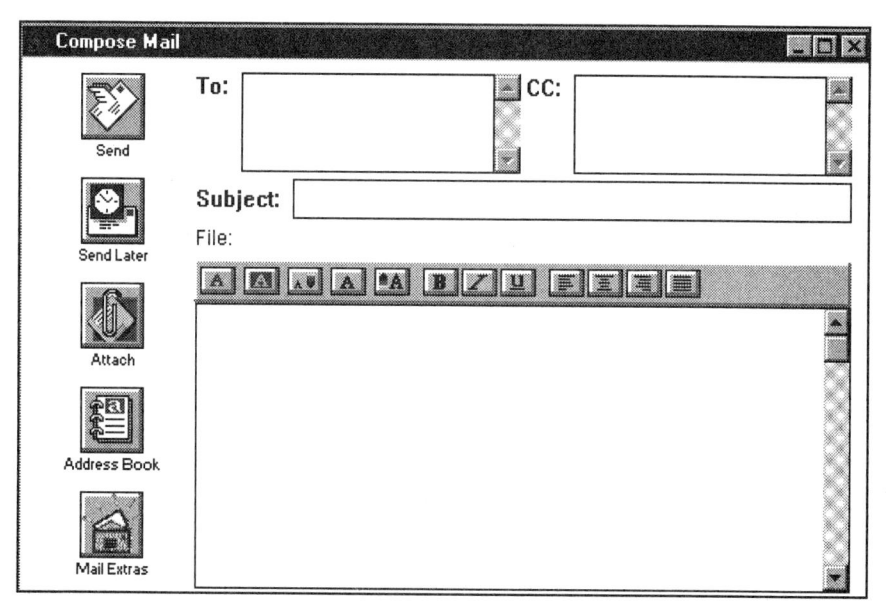

- Fill in the e-mail address(es) in the To box of the Compose Mail screen.

OR

- Select Address Book and double-click to select an address. (See Page 226 for more information on your Address book.)
- If you are sending the same message to multiple recipients, fill in the CC: (Carbon Copy) box with the e-mail addresses of recipients who will receive a copy of this message. These names will display to all recipients of the message.
- If you want to send BCC: (Blind courtesy copies—copies of a message sent to others but whose names are not visible to the main or other recipients), put the address in parenthesis, for example: (ddcpub.com).

√ *Multiple addresses must be separated with a comma.*

- Fill in the Subject box with a one-line summary of your message. AOL will not deliver a message without a subject heading.
- Fill in the body of the message.

Send Messages

- Click the Send button [Send] to send the message immediately.

OR

- Click the Send Later button [Send Later] to send a message later that you have composed offline.

Reply to Mail

- You can reply to mail messages while online or compose replies to e-mail offline to send later.
- To reply to e-mail:

  - Click the Reply button [Reply] from the displayed message screen. If the message has been sent to more than one person, you can send your response to each recipient of the message by clicking the Reply to All button [Reply to All]. The addresses of the sender and, if desired, all recipients will be automatically inserted into the address fields.

    √ To include part or all of the original message in your Reply, select the contents of the original message to be included in quotes in your message and click the Reply button to begin your reply.

  - Click the Send button [Send] if you are online and want to send the reply immediately or click the Send Later button [Send Later].

Forward Mail

- There are times when you may want to send mail sent to you on to someone else.
- To forward e-mail:

  - Click the Forward button [Forward] from the displayed message screen and fill in the address(es) of the recipients of the forwarded message.

  - Click the Send button [Send] if you are online and want to send the reply immediately or click the Send Later button [Send Later].

AOL Mail Help

  - For answers to many of your basic e-mail questions, click Mail, Mail Center, and click on the Let's Get Started button.

America Online E-mail: 8

◆ Add Attachments to a Message ◆ Download File Attachments

Add Attachments to a Message

- You can attach a file to send along with any e-mail message. Before you send a file attachment—especially if it is a multimedia file—it is a good idea to make sure that the recipient's e-mail program can read the attachment.

To attach files to a message:

- Compose the message to be sent.
- Click the Attach button [Attach] on the Compose Message screen.
- Select the drive and folder where the file you wish to attach is located.
- Double-click the file to attach from the Attach File dialog box.

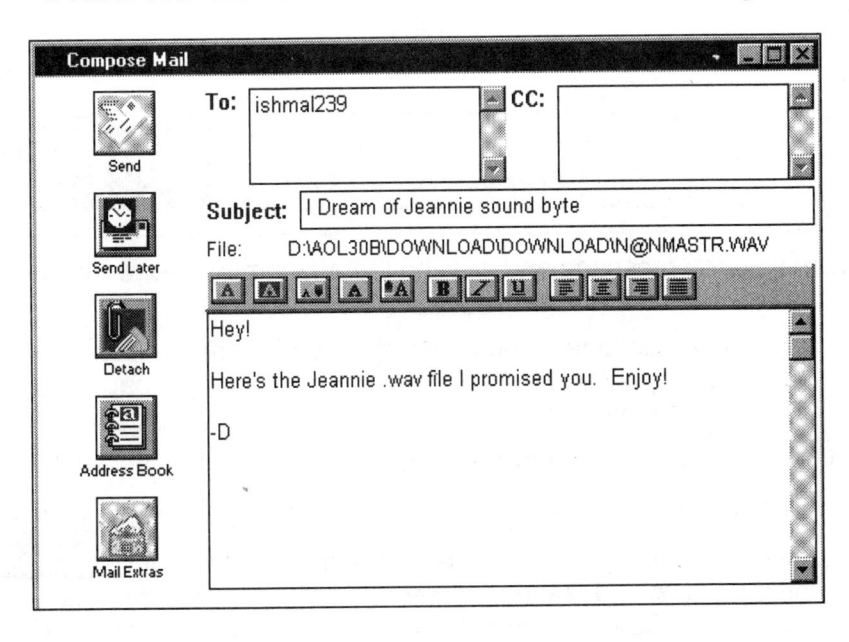

America Online E-mail 223

- If you are online, click the Send button [Send] to send the message immediately, or click the Send Later button [Send Later] to store the message in your Outgoing Mail if you are working offline.

√ *Multiple files must be grouped together in a single archive using a file compression program such as PKZIP or WINZIP. Both you and the recipient will need a file compression program.*

Download E-mail File Attachments

- An e-mail message that arrives with a file attachment is displayed in your new mail list with a small diskette under the message icon.

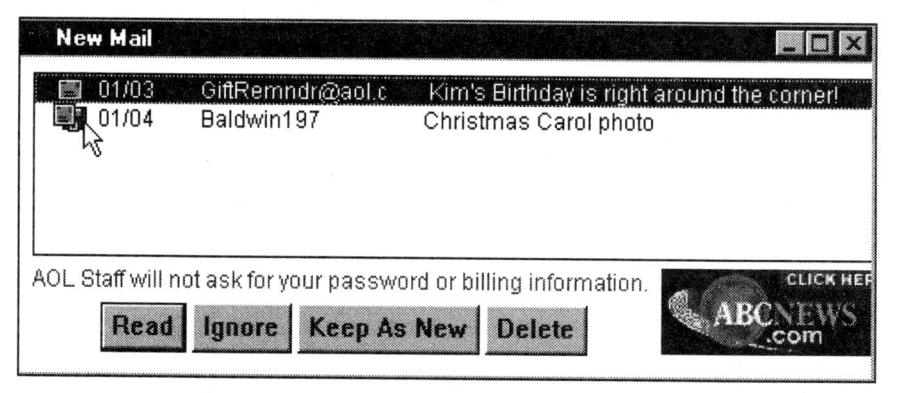

New Mail			
01/03	GiftRemndr@aol.c	Kim's Birthday is right around the corner!
01/04	Baldwin197	Christmas Carol photo

AOL Staff will not ask for your password or billing information.

[Read] [Ignore] [Keep As New] [Delete]

- Opening the message and viewing the attachment are two separate steps:
  - Open the message by double-clicking on it from the New Mail list (see "To display and read new and unread mail" on page 219). The message will display.
  - You can choose to download the file attachment immediately by clicking the Download File button [Download File] at the bottom of the displayed message screen. Click the Save button [Save] on the Download Manager screen to save the file, by default, to the AOL30/Download folder. If you desire, you can change the save destination folder.

- A status box will display while the attachment is being downloaded or transferred to your computer.

- At the end of the download, the file transfer box will close and you will see the message "File's Done."

OR

- You may choose to download the file later. Click the Download Later button **Download Later** to store the message in the Download Manager. When you are ready to download the file, click File, Download Manager, and then select the file to download. You must be online.

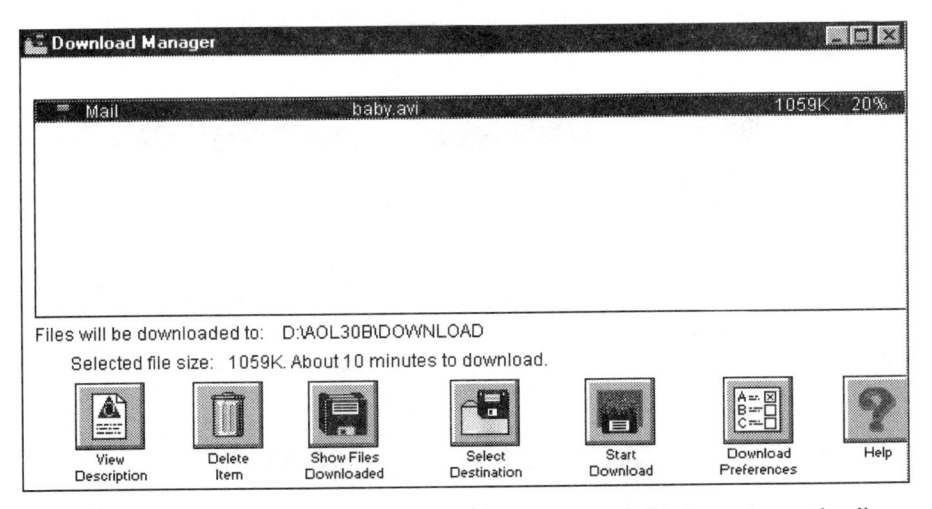

√ Click Sign off after transfer if you want AOL to automatically disconnect when the transfer is complete.

To change the default location of where files are stored:

- Click the Select Destination button from the Download Manager screen and choose the desired destination from the Select Path dialog box.

America Online E-mail 225

America Online E-mail: 9

♦ **Add Entries to the Address Book**
♦ **Enter an Address Using the Address Book**

Add Entries to the Address Book

- An easy way to keep track of e-mail addresses is to enter them into the Address Book. Once an e-mail address entry has been created, you can automatically insert it from the Address Book into the address fields.

To create Address Book entries:

- Click <u>M</u>ail, Edit <u>A</u>ddress Book. The Address Book dialog box displays.

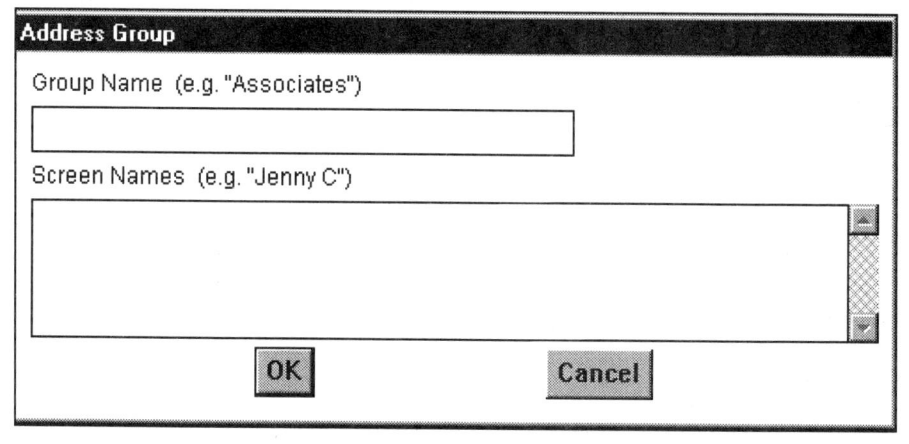

- Click the Create button [Create] to open the Address Group box.

Address Group

Group Name (e.g. "Associates")

Screen Names (e.g. "Jenny C")

[OK]   [Cancel]

- Enter the real name or nickname of the e-mail recipient (e.g., JohnV) or the name of a Group listing (e.g., Book Club) in the Group Name box. The name you enter in this box is the name that will appear in the Address Book list.

- Press the Tab key to move to the Screen Names box and enter the complete e-mail address of the recipient or the e-mail addresses of everyone in the group listing. When entering multiple addresses such as in a group listing, each address must be separated by a comma.

- Click OK.
- √ *When sending mail to AOL members through AOL, you do not need to enter the @aol.com domain information. Enter only their screen name as the e-mail address. For all other Address Book entries you must enter the entire address.*

Delete an Address Book Entry

- Click Mail, Edit Address Book to open the Address Book.
- Click the name to delete.
- Click the Delete button **Delete**.
- Click Yes.
- Click OK to close the Address Book.

Enter an Address Using the Address Book

- Place the cursor in the desired address field.
- Click the Address Book button [Address Book] to open the Address Book.
- Double-click the name or names from the Address Book list to insert in the TO: or CC: address box and click OK.

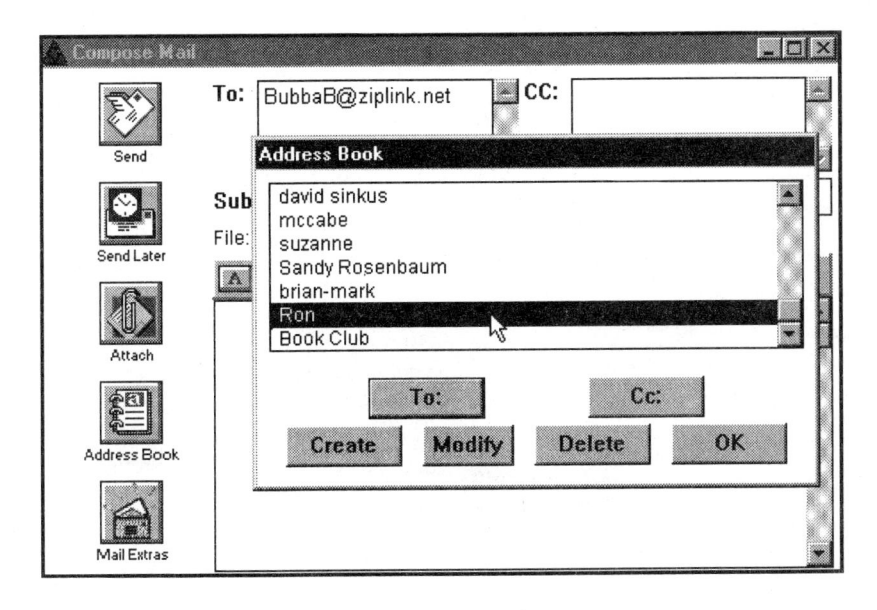

Index

A

a
  before acronyms 9-10
  vs. his, her or their to avoid
    sexist writing 131
a lot 1
a.m. 2
Abbreviations 1-4
  apostrophe with 2, 30
  Latin 4, 93
  of dates 63
accept vs. except 5
Acronyms 1, 6-10
Action words. See Verbs
  infinitive form of 16
  parallel structure with 123-124
Active voice 11-20
Address book
  Netscape Messenger 190
  Outlook Express 205
  America Online 226, 227
Adjectives
  compound 88-89
  parallel structure with 123-124
Adverbs
  hyphen with 91
  quickly 133
advice vs. advise 20
affect vs. effect 21-22
affective 22
after 47-48, 83-84
Agreement
  pronoun and antecedent 130
  subject and verb 150-159
Alignment
  memos 109
  lists 105
all ready vs. already 23
all right 23
along with, subject-verb agreement ... 155
also, in run-on sentences 140
although 47-49
  vs. however 87
America Online
  add attachments 223

address book 226
Attach button 223
change default location 225
compose mail 219
Compose Mail button 219
delete address book entry 227
download attachment 224
Forward button 222
forward mail 222
Let's Get Started button 222
mail help 222
read new mail 219
Reply button 221
Reply to All button 221
reply to mail 221
send a message 221
Send button 221, 222
Send Later button 221, 222
using address book entry 227
You Have Mail button 219
among vs. between 23
amongst 23
amount vs. number 24
an, before acronyms 9-10
and
  comma with 50-51, 53
  to correct run-on sentences 141
  vs. as well as 31-32
anxious vs. eager 25
anyone 130
  subject-verb agreement 153-154
Apostrophe 26-30
  abbreviations 2, 30
  acronyms 7-8
  contractions 30-31
  possessive form 26-30, 132, 166
  possessive pronouns 132, 169
Appositive, comma with 49
are, subject-verb agreement 152-153
as follows, before a list 104
as well as 31-32
  subject-verb agreement 32, 155
as 47-49
assure vs. ensure and insure 33-34
Attachments
  America Online 223, 224

228

Index

Netscape Messenger 192, 194, 195
Outlook Express 217, 218
Attention lines 35
autumn, capitalization of 43

B

bcc 45
because 35-36, 47-48
before 47-48, 83-84
being that 37
being 164
Best regards
  in complimentary closings 54-55
between vs. among 23
between you and me 107
bi 37
biannual 37
Binary files 192
black, capitalization of 70
blind carbon copy 45
board 38
Boldface
  emphasis 94
  headings 84-85
  reference/subject lines 138
  vs. capitalization 44
Bookmark a message
  Netscape Messenger 184
Bullets 104
but not
  subject-verb agreement 155
but
  comma with 53
  to correct run-on sentences 141

C

cannot and can't 38
Capitalization 39-44
  for emphasis 44
  in e-mail 44, 66
  in lists 105-106
  in reference/subject lines 137-138
  of black 70
  of board 38
  of centuries 84
  of complimentary closings 54-55
  of ethnic groups 70
  of headings 44, 85
  of nationalities 70
  of races 70
  of white 70

  vs. boldface 44
  vs. italics 44
Carbon copy 45
cc 45
  spacing of in letters 98-99
  placement of in memos 108
Centuries
  capitalization of 64
  hyphen with 92
  nd, rd, st or th with 118-119
Churchill, Winston 128
Clauses 161-163
  introductory 47
  subordinate 36, 47-49
Closings. See Complimentary closings.
Colon 46
  after opening of memos 108-109
  in salutations 120, 143
  vs. dash 59-60
  vs. semicolon 147
  with quotation marks 136
  with reference/subject lines 137
Comma 47-53
  after opening of memos 108-109
  in complimentary closings .. 54-55, 120
  in lists 51-52, 106
  in run-on sentences 140-142
  in salutations 143
  vs. dash 59-60
  with and 50-51, 53
  with appositive 49
  with as well as 31-32
  with because 35
  with but 53
  with dates 62-63
  with e.g. 4, 93
  with i.e. 4, 93
  with parentheses 127
  with quotation marks 135
  with that 161-162
  with which 162
Comma fault 140
Comma splice 140
committee, subject-verb agreement ... 156
complementary vs. complimentary 56
Complimentary closings 54-55
  in e-mail 68
  in letters 97
  with no salutation 144-145
  open punctuation with 55, 120
Compose a message
  America Online 219

Internet in an Hour Business Communication and E-Mail   229

Netscape Messenger...................... 185
Outlook Express 205
Compound adjectives, hyphen 88-89
Compound nouns 89
Contractions 57-58
   apostrophe........................... 26, 30-31
   can't 38
   it's 95-96
   who's... 166
   you're 168-169

D

Dangling modifier.......................... 111-113
Dash 59-61
data, subject-verb agreement..... 156-157
Dates 62-64
   apostrophe to omit numbers............ 30
   comma after.................................... 53
Decades
   apostrophe with 26-27, 64
   plural of.. 64
Default save location, change in America
   Online 225
Degrees, abbreviations for 2
Delete a message
   Netscape Messenger...................... 183
   Outlook Express 203
Departments, capitalization of 39-41
despite 47-48
different from vs. different than 65-66
Directions
   active voice............................... 18-19
   capitalization of............................... 43
District of Columbia, abbreviation of 3
Dollars
   alignment of in vertical lists............ 105
   as words or figures 115-117
   decimal point 116
   in lists... 116
   mixing with other numbers....... 116-117
Download attachment
   America Online.............................. 224
Dr., in salutation 146
Drafts folder
   Outlook Express 208
during... 47-48

E

E-mail 66-68
   capitaliation in 44, 66-67
   reference/subject lines............. 68, 139

run-on sentences............................140
shouting......................................44, 67
e.g. 4, 93
each..130
   subject-verb agreement...... 74-75, 154
eager vs. anxious 25
east, capitalization of 43
Edit message drafts
   Outlook Express 208
effect vs. affect 21-22
effective 22
Ellipsis 69
Em dash 60-61
En dash 60-61
enclosed 152
ensure vs. assure and insure 33-34
Esq. 146
etc. 2
Ethnic groups
   capitalization of................................70
   hyphen with 70, 92
everyone..130
   subject-verb agreement.......... 153-154
except vs. accept.................................5
Exclamation point 71
   with quotation marks 136

F

fall, capitalization of 43
farther vs. further................................72
fewer vs. less....................................73
File attachments, see Attachments.
Financial terms, hyphen 91
Flaming, in e-mail 67
follow-up vs. follow up 88-89
Fonts.. 74-75
   combining 74-75
   in headings 74, 84-85
   sans serif 74, 85
   serif...74, 85
formally vs. formerly 76
Format
   e-mail messages 66-67
   letters.................................... 97-103
   memos 108-109
   paragraphs 120-122
   reference/subject lines 137-138
Forward a message
   America Online.............................222
   Netscape Messenger 188
   Outlook Express 210
Fragments 77

Index

G

Geographic regions, capitalization of .. 43
Gerunds
   parallel structure with 123-124
   preceded by your 167
Get Msg
   Netscape Messenger 181, 182
graduated, vs. was graduated 77
group, subject-verb agreement 156

H

had 81
has 78-81
   speaking errors with 81
   subject-verb agreement 152-153
have 78-81
   subject-verb agreement 152-153
he 82-84, 130
he/she 131-132
Headings 84-85
   all caps 44, 85
   sans serif font 74, 85
   typefaces 74, 84-85
her 82-84, 130, 132
hers 26-27, 132
him 82-84
his 26-27, 130-132
his/her 131-132
hopefully 86
however 87
   in run-on sentences 141-142
Hyphen 88-89
   in numbers 70, 91-92
   vs. dash 46
   with bi 37
   with ethnic groups, races
      and nationalities 70, 92
   with semi 37

I

I vs. me and myself 107
i.e. 4, 93
Identity settings
   Netscape Messenger 178
if 47-48
imply vs. infer 93
in addition to
   subject-verb agreement 155
in effect 22

Index Card icon
   Outlook Express 205
Infinitives
   split 149
   to change passive voice
      to active voice 16
ing words 167
   See also Gerunds.
Insert address
   Netscape Messenger 190
   Outlook Express 213
Inside address, in letters 97-98
insure 33
Internet Connection Wizard
   Outlook Express 195
Interrupters
   comma with 49-50
   subject-verb agreement 155
into effect 22
Introductory clauses or phrases
   comma with 47-49
is, subject-verb agreement 152-153
it, agreement with antecedent 130
Italics 94
   in headings 8
   in reference/subject lines 138
   vs. capitalization 44, 94
   vs. underlining 94
   vs. upper case 44, 94
Items in a series, comma with 50-52
its 26-27, 130-134
   vs. it's 95-96

J

Jefferson, Thomas 39
Joint possession
   apostrophe to show 29-30

L

Latin abbreviations, e.g. and i.e. 4, 93
less vs. fewer 73
Letters 97-103
   attention lines 35
   no salutation 143-145
   reference lines 99, 137-139
   salutations 97, 143-146
   subject lines 137-139
   with headings 84-85
Lists 104-106
   colon before 46
   comma 51-52, 105-106

Internet in an Hour Business Communication and E-Mail   231

dollars 116
of paragraphs 121-122
of sentences 125
parallelism 104, 124-125
loan vs. lend 96
Locations, capitalization of 43

M

Mail Folder list
   Outlook Express 198, 200
Mail help
   America Online 222
Mail icon
   Outlook Express 197
Mail Server
   Netscape Messenger..................... 179
Mail toolbar
   Outlook Express 201
Mail window
   Outlook Express 199
Margins, in letters 99
me vs. I and myself............................ 107
Memos 108-110
   complimentary closings 55
   reference/subject lines.... 108, 137-139
Message
   compose in Outlook Express 205
   delete in Outlook Express.............. 203
   forward in America Online 222
   forward in Netscape Messenger.... 188
   Forward in Outlook Express 210
   get new in Netscape Messenger ... 182
   print in Outlook Express 203
   read in America Online 219
   read in Netscape Messenger......... 182
   read in Outlook Express 201
   reply in America Online 221
   reply in Outlook Express................ 209
   reply to in Netscape Messenger.... 187
   retrieve in Outlook Express 199
   save in Outlook Express................ 204
   send in America Online 221
   send in Netscape Messenger........ 186
   send in Outlook Express 206
mid, in hyphenated words 90
mine 132
Modifier, danging or misplaced 111-113
Monospaced fonts 74-75
Ms., in salutation......................... 145-146
multi, in hyphenated words 91
my 132
myself vs. I and me............................ 107

N

Nationalities 70
   hyphen with 70, 92
nd
   with centuries 117-118
   with dates 63-64
   with numbers 118-119
Netscape Messenger
   Address button 185, 188, 191
   Attach button 195
   attach files 194
   bookmark a message 184
   Close button 191
   compose a message 185
   configure....................................... 178
   delete a message 183
   Delete button 181, 183
   File attachments 192
   File button..................................... 181
   Forward a message...................... 188
   Forward button 181, 188
   Get Msg................................181, 182
   get new Message 182
   identity settings............................. 178
   Insert an address.......................... 190
   Mail Server 179
   Message Composition toolbar........ 187
   Message Composition window....... 185
   Message List window 180
   New Card button 189
   New Msg button 190
   Next button 181, 182
   Paperclip icon............................... 192
   print a message............................ 183
   Print button 181, 183
   Quote button 188
   read a message............................ 182
   Reply to a message...................... 187
   save attached file 194
   Save button 187
   Security button 181, 187
   send a message 186
   Send button 187
   Spelling button.......................186, 187
   start 180
   Stop button 187
   View attachments 192
Netscape
   Personal address book.................. 189
non, in hyphenated words 90
none...114
   subject-verb agreement.......... 114, 158

232

Index

Nonrestrictive clauses 161-163
nor, subject-verb agreement 155
north, capitalization of..................... 43
notice of hours, days or weeks 28-29
Nouns
   pronouns to take the place of 130
   with different from 65
number
   subject-verb agreement................. 157
   vs. amount 24
Numbers 115-119
   alignment of in vertical lists............ 105
   hyphen.................................... 91, 118
   with headings 84-85

O

Object
   her/him as 82-84
   me as... 107
   whom as 165
of vs. have 82
one
   as pronoun............................. 131-132
   subject-verb agreement.......... 153-154
Open punctuation 120
   with complimentary closings............ 55
or
   comma with 53
   subject-verb agreement.......... 154-155
our 132
ours................................... 26-27, 132
Outbox folder
   Outlook Express 207
Outlook Express
   Address Book button 205
   attach a file 218
   attachment icon 217, 218
   Column headings........................... 200
   compose a message 205
   configure....................................... 195
   delete a message 203
   Delete button on Message toolbar. 203
   Drafts folder................................. 208
   edit message drafts 208
   forward a message 210
   Forward Message button............... 210
   Index Card icon 205
   insert address from address book . 213
   Internet Connection Wizard........... 195
   Mail Folder list 198, 200
   Mail icon 197
   Mail toolbar 201
   Mail toolbar Delete button 203
   mail window..................................199
   message list pane 200
   New Mail Message button 205
   Next button 202
   Outbox folder................................207
   paperclip icon 215
   Personal address BOOK 211
   print a message 203
   Print button 204
   read a message.............................201
   Read Mail shortcut 200
   reply to a message 209
   Reply to All button 209
   retrieve new messages 199
   save a message 204
   save a message in Outbox folder...208
   save an attached file 218
   send a message 206
   send a message from Outbox
      folder 208
   Send and Receive button 208
   Send button 211
   send message drafts 208
   Sent Items folder 208
   shortcuts......................................198
   start 197
   store a message in Outbox folder ..207
   view attached files 215

P

p.m. 1
Paperclip icon
   Netscape Messenger 192
   Outlook Express 215
Paragraphs................................ 120-122
Parallelism................................. 123-125
   in lists 104, 124-125
Parentheses 126-127
   with acronyms 7-8
   with numbers 118-119
Passive voice 11-20, 77
   changing to active voice 15-18
Past perfect tense 81
Percents
   as words or figures 115-117
   in vertical lists 104-105
Period
   in lists 106
   with abbreviations............................ 2-4
   with parentheses 127
   with quotation marks 135

Internet in an Hour Business Communication and E-Mail

Personal address book
   Netscape 189
   Outlook Express 211
Personal titles, capitalization of 42
Place phrases, comma after 52-53
Places, capitalization of 39-41
Plurals
   errors with apostrophes 26-27
   of abbreviations 2
   of acronyms 8
   of decade 64
   of pronouns 130-132
   possessive form of 27-28
   to avoid sexist writing 131-132
   use of apostrophe to form 30
Possessive form
   apostrophe 26-30
   its 95-96
   of abbreviations 3
   of acronyms 7-8
   of plurals 35-36
   of pronouns 166
   whose 26-27, 132, 166
   with different from 65
   your 168-169
Postal abbreviations 3
Prefixes
   bi 37
   hyphen after 89-91
   mid 90
   multi 91
   non 90
   re 90
   semi 37
Prepositional phrases .. 150-151, 152-155
Prepositions 128
   in between you and me 107
   in modifying phrases 113
   who or whom after 165
   with pronouns 83-84
Present perfect tense 78-81
principal vs. principle 129
Print a message
   Netscape Messenger 183
   Outlook Express 203
Procedures, active voice 18-19
Programs, capitalization of 39-41
Projects, capitalization of 39-41
Pronouns 130-132
   See also specific pronouns: anyone,
   each, everyone, he, her, hers, him, his,
   I, it, its, me, mine, my, myself, none,
   one, our, ours, she, their, theirs, them,
   these, they, this, us, we, who, whom,
   whose, you, your, yours.
   as objects or subjects 82-83
   apostrophes with 26-27
   verb agreement 153-154
   with different from 65
   with ing words (gerunds) 167
Proportional fonts 74-75
Punctuation.
   See specific marks of punctuation.
   in lists 105-106
   open 120
   quotation marks 134-136
   semicolon 141-142
   with parentheses 127

Q

Question mark
   with quotation marks 136
quickly vs. quicker 133
Quotation, ellipsis with 69
Quotation marks 134-136

R

Races 70
   capitalization of 70
   hyphen with 70, 92
rd
   with centuries 118
   with dates 63
   with numbers 118
re
   in hyphenated words 90
Read a message
   America Online 219
   Netscape Messenger 182
   Outlook Express 199-201
Recommendations
   active voice 19-20
Reference lines 137-139
   in e-mail 68, 139
   in memos 108
Regards
   in complimentary closings 55
   in e-mail 68
Reply to a message
   America Online 221
   Netscape Messenger 187
   Outlook Express 209
   Outlook Express 208

Index

Respectfully
   in complimentary closings 54
Restrictive clauses 161-163
Restrictive expressions
   comma with 50
Run-on sentences 140-142

S

Salutations 143-146
   colon after 46, 120, 143
   in e-mail 68
   in letters 97
Sans serif fonts 74
Seasons, capitalization of 43
semi
   hyphen with 37
   vs. bi 37
Semicolon 147
   in vertical lists 105-106, 147
   to correct run-on sentences.... 141-142
   with however 87
   with quotation marks 136
Sent Items folder
   Outlook Express 208
Sentence fragments 77
Sentence length 148
   effect of semicolon on 147
Sentences
   ending with a preposition 128
   list of 104-106, 125
   numbers at beginning of 115
   parallel structure of 123-124
   parentheses within 126-127
   run-on. See Run-on sentences.
   spacing between 74
Serif fonts 74
Sexist writing 131-132
she 82-84, 130
Shortcuts
   Outlook Express 198
since 47-49
Sincerely, in complimentary closings ... 54
Slashes, in dates 64
Small caps, in abbreviations 1
south, capitalization of 43
Spacing
   around paragraphs 121-122
   between paragraphs 120-121
   between sentences 74
Spelling button
   Netscape Messenger 186, 187
Split infinitives 149

spring, capitalization of 43
st
   with centuries 118-119
   with dates 63-64
   with numbers 118-119
Start
   Netscape Messenger 180
   Outlook Express 197
States, abbreviation of 3
Stop button
   Netscape Messenger 187
Store a message
   Outbox folder in Outlook Express...207
Subject lines 137-139
   in memos 108
Subject
   agreement with verb 150-159
   he/she as 82-83
   I as 107
Subject-verb agreement 150-159
   with as well as 32, 155
   with board 38
   with none 114, 158
Subordinate clauses
   comma with 36, 47-49
   subject-verb agreement 158-159
   with that omitted 159
such as, colon with 46
summer, capitalization of 43
supposed to 160

T

team, subject-verb agreement 156
Tense
   effect on meaning 78-79
   errors with 80-81
   parallelism of 123-124
   past perfect 81
   present perfect 78-81
   switching 79
   vs. voice 18
th
   with centuries 118-119
   with dates 63-64
   with numbers 118-119
than
   parallel structure with 124
   vs. then 160
   with different 65-66
   with pronouns 83-84
Thanks
   in e-mail 68

that 161-163
   subject-verb agreement 202
   vs. which 126-127
   vs. who 162
   vs. whom 162
the vs. his, her or their 131-132
the following, before lists 104-106
the reason being 164
the reason is because 36
their 130, 132
theirs 26-27, 132
them 130
then vs. than 161-162
there, to start a sentence 151-152
therefore, in run-on sentences 141-142
these 130
they 130
this 130
Time phrases, comma with 52-53
Titles 42-44, 94
to 47-48
together with
   subject-verb agreement 155
total, subject-verb agreement 157-158
Transition words or phrases
   comma with 49
Type size 75
Typefaces. See also Fonts.

U

Underlining
   for emphasis 94
   of headings 110
   of reference/subject lines 138
   vs. italics 122
Upper case. See Capitalization.
   vs. italics 122
us 130
used to 165

V

variety, subject-verb agreement 157
Verbs
   active voice 11-20
   agreement with subject 150-159
   being 164
   being that 37
   helping 78-81
   in lists 104
   parallel structure with 123-124

passive voice 11-20, 77
tense vs. voice 18
Very truly yours 54
View attached files
   Outlook Express 215
   Netscape Messenger 192

W

was, subject-verb agreement 152-153
was graduated vs. graduated 77
we 130
were, subject-verb agreement ... 152-153
west, capitalization of 43
when 47-48
which 77
   and parenthetical thoughts 162
   comma with 162
   eliminating to increase clarity 163
   subject-verb agreement 202
   vs. that 161-163
while 37
white, capitalization of 70
who vs. that 162
   vs. whom 211
whom vs. that 162
   vs. who 211
whose 26-27, 132
   vs. who's 166
winter, capitalization of 43
With warmest regards
   in complimentary closings 54
Word division 92
   at end of page 100

Y

you
   to avoid sexist writing 131-132
   with ing words (gerunds) 167
You Have Mail button
   America Online 219
your 132
   vs. you're 168-169
   with ing words (gerunds) 167
you're
   vs. your 168-169
yours 26-27, 132
Yours truly
   in complimentary closings 54

Our One-Day Course has you using your software the next day

$18 ea.
Includes diskette

Here's how we do it
We struck out all the unnecessary words that don't teach anything. No introductory nonsense. We get right to the point-in "See spot run" language. No polysyllabic verbiage. We give you the keystrokes and the illustrated layout; step by simple step.

You learn faster because you read less
No fairy tales, novels, or literature. Small words, fewer words, short sentences, and fewer of them. We pen every word as if an idiot had to read it. You understand it faster because it reads easier.

Illustrated exercises show you how
We tell you, show you, and explain what you see. The layout shows you what we just explained. The answers fly off the page and into your brain as if written on invisible glass. No narration or exposition. No time wasted. **Each book comes with a practice disk to eliminate typing the exercises.**

DID WE MAKE ONE FOR YOU?

Cat. No.	Title
C-2	Access 97, Day 1 ISBN 1-56243-519-1
C-29	Access 97, Day 2 ISBN 1-56243-579-5
C-30	Access 97, Day 3 ISBN 1-56243-580-9
C-1	Access 7 for Windows 95 ISBN 1-56243-518-3
C-23	Creating a Web Page w/Word 97
C-4	Excel 97, Day 1 ISBN 1-56243-521-3
C-27	Excel 97, Day 2 ISBN 1-56243-577-9
C-28	Excel 97, Day 3 ISBN 1-56243-578-7
C-3	Excel 7 for Windows 95 ISBN 1-56243-520-5
C-22	FrontPage w/Sim. CD ISBN 1-56243-448-9
C-5	Internet E-mail & FTP w/Sim. CD
C-6	Intro to Computers and Windows 95 ISBN 1-56243-523-X
C-21	Local Area Network ISBN 1-56243-502-7
C-35	Lotus Notes 4.5 ISBN 1-56243-589-2
C-7	Macintosh System 7.5 ISBN 1-56243-524-8
C-8	MS Explorer w/ Sim. CD ISBN 1-56243-525-6
C-9	MS Project 4 ISBN 1-56243-526-4
C-10	Netscape Navigator w/ Sim. CD
C-11	Outlook 97, Day 1 ISBN 1-56243-528-0
C-32	Outlook 97, Day 2 ISBN 1-56243-582-5
C-12	PageMaker 5 ISBN 1-56243-529-9
C-14	PowerPoint 97, Day 1 ISBN 1-56243-531-0
C-31	PowerPoint 97, Day 2 ISBN 1-56243-581-7
C-13	PowerPoint 7 for Windows 95
C-16	Windows 95 ISBN 1-56243-533-7
C-24	Windows NT 4.0 ISBN 1-56243-297-4
C-15	Windows NT 3.5 ISBN 1-56243-532-9
C-18	Word 97, Day 1 ISBN 1-56243-535-3
C-25	Word 97, Day 2 ISBN 1-56243-575-2
C-26	Word 97, Day 3 ISBN 1-56243-576-0
C-17	Word 7 for Windows 95 ISBN 1-56243-534-5
C-19	WordPerfect 6.1 ISBN 1-56243-536-1
C-34	Upgrading to Office 97 ISBN 1-56243-588-4
C-20	Visual Basic 3.0 ISBN 1-56243-537-X

6/98 OD

There's so much on the Web yet to discover ...
Our Internet-In-An-Hour Series helps you find i

Each of four different books gives you the basics of Internet usage, then introduces you to a world of practical World Wide Web sites, searching tip: and advice on browsing—all relating to the book's particular subject matt

Internet in an Hour FOR STUDENTS
- Use Online College Applications
- Secure Financial Aid
- Discover Homework Resources
- Put Your Resume on the Internet
- Find Employment

Cat. No. HR1
ISBN 1-56243-601-5

Internet in an Hour FOR SALES PEOPLE
- Develop Sales Leads
- Prepare for Sales Calls
- Stay Ahead of Your Competition
- Plan Business Travel
- Research New Markets

Cat. No. HR4
ISBN 1-56243-604-X

Internet in an Hour FOR MANAGERS
- Find New Customers
- Cut Operating Expenses
- Solve Personnel Problems
- Manage Your Time
- Make Your Staff More Efficient

Cat. No. HR2
ISBN 1-56243-602-3

Internet in an Ho FOR BEGINNERS
- Learn Internet Bas
- Shop Online
- Make Travel Plans
- Manage Your Finar
- Explore Arts & Entertainment

Cat. No. HR3
ISBN 1-56243-603-1

$10 ea

To order call 800-528-3897 or fax 800-528-386 Visit our Web site: http://www.ddcpub.c

DDC *Publishing*

275 Madison Ave. New York, NY 10
9/9

DDC Quick Reference Guides
find software answers faster
because you read less

Find it quickly and get back to the keyboard—fast

The index becomes your quick locator. Just follow the step-by-step illustrated instructions. We tell you what to do in five or six words. Sometimes only two. No narration or exposition. Just "press this—type that" illustrated commands. The spiral binding keeps pages open so you can type what you read. You save countless hours of lost time by locating the illustrated answer in seconds.

The time you save when this guide goes to work for you will pay for it the very first day

$12 ea.

Did We Make One for You?

TITLE	CAT.No
ss 2 for Windows	OAX2
ss 7 for Windows 95	AX95
ss 97	G28
Works 5 for Macintosh	G39
uter Terms	D18
WordPerfect Suite 8	G32
WordPerfect 7 Win 95	G12
WordPerfect Suite 7 r Win 95	G11
5	J17
6.0 - 6.22	ODS62
5 for Windows	F18
7 for Windows 95	XL7
97	G27
et, 2nd Edition	I217
1-2-3 Rel. 3.1 DOS	J18
1-2-3 Rel. 3.4 DOS	L317
1-2-3 Rel. 4 DOS	G4
1-2-3 Rel. 4 Win	O3013
1-2-3 Rel. 5 Win	L19
1-2-3 Rel. 6 Win 95	G13
Notes 4.5	G15
Smart Suite 97	G34

TITLE	CAT.No
Office for Win. 3.1	M017
Office for Win 95	M095
Office 97	G25
PageMaker 5 for Win & Mac	PM18
PowerPoint 4 for Win	OPPW4
PowerPoint 7 for Win 95	PPW7
PowerPoint 97	G31
Quattro Pro 6 for Win	QPW6
Quicken 4 for Windows	G7
Windows NT 4	G16
Windows 3.1 & 3.11	N317
Windows 95	G6
Windows 98	G35
Word 6 for Windows	OWDW6
Word 7 for Windows 95	WDW7
Word 97	G26
WordPerfect 5.1+ for DOS	W-5.1
WordPerfect 6 for DOS	W18
WordPerfect 6 for Win	OWPW6
WordPerfect 6.1 for Win	W19
Works 3 for DOS	M18
Works 3 for Win	OWKW3
Works 4 for Win 95	WKW4

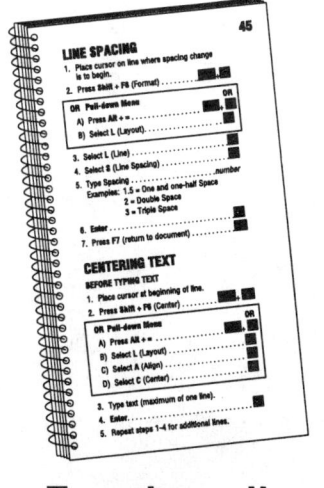

To order call
800-528-3897
or fax 800-528-3862
Visit our Web site:
http://www.ddcpub.com

DDC Publishing
275 Madison Ave., New York, NY 10016

9/98 Q

Fast-teach Learning Books

How we designed each book

Our self-paced hands-on text gives you the concept and the objective in simple language. We show you how to format the exercise. Next to the exercise we provide the keystrokes and the illustrated layout; step by simple step - graded and cumulative.

If a word didn't tell, it got tossed out. We don't teach reading. You go into software functi immediately. No time wasted.

Did we make one for you? $27 ea

Title	Cat. No.	Title	Ca
Creating a Web Page w/ Office 97	Z23	Lotus 1-2-3 Rel. 4 & 5 for Windows	
Corel Office 7	Z12	Microsoft Office 97	
Corel WordPerfect 7	Z16	Microsoft Office for Windows 95	
Corel WordPerfect 8	Z31	PowerPoint 97	
DOS + Windows	Z7	Typing with Microsoft Word 97	
Excel 97	Z21	Windows 3.1 – A Quick Study	W
Excel 5 for Windows	E9	Windows 95	
Excel 7 for Windows 95	Z11	Windows 98	
Internet	Z15	Word 97	
Internet for Business	Z27	Word 6 for Windows	1-W
Internet for Kids	Z25	Word 7 for Windows 95	
Keyboarding/Word Processing for Kids	Z33	WordPerfect 6 for Windows	
Lotus 1-2-3 Rel. 2.2–4.0 for DOS	L9	WordPerfect 6.1 for Windows	
		Works 4 for Windows 95	

Learning the Internet
We teach you how to get information from the Internet. Includes CD-ROM Simulation.
$27
Cat. No. Z30

Learning Keyboarding & Word Processing Microsoft® Word 97
It does exactly wh tells you.
$27
Cat. No. Z24

Learning the Internet for Business
From email to online business resources, Web marketing to a list of essential downloads. This book covers it all.
$27
Cat. No. Z27

Learning the Internet for Kids
Kids sail the seve and learn how to the Internet, send download and bro the Internet.
$27
Cat. No. Z25

DDC Publishing
275 Madison Avenue, New York, NY 10016

**Phone: 800-528-389
Fax 800-528-380**